Popul

South-Central Okanagan
Kelowna | Penticton | Oliver

Gerry Shea

RMB

Rocky Mountain Books

www.rmbooks.com

Library and Archives Canada Cataloguing in Publication

Shea, Gerry, author
    South-Central Okanagan : Kelowna, Penticton, Oliver / Gerry Shea.

(Popular day hikes ; 5)
Issued in print and electronic formats.
ISBN 978-1-77160-088-0 (pbk.).—ISBN 978-1-77160-089-7 (epub).—
ISBN 978-1-77160-090-3 (pdf)

    1. Trails—British Columbia—Okanagan Valley (Region)—Guidebooks. 2. Hiking—British Columbia—Okanagan Valley (Region)—Guidebooks. 3. Okanagan Valley (B.C. : Region)—Guidebooks. I. Title. II. Series: Popular day hikes ; 5

GV199.44.C22B748374 2015   796.5109711'5   C2015-901010-1
                                                   C2015-901011-X

Front cover photo: Glorious Sunset, Lake Landscape © Arpad Benedek

Back cover photo: On the way to the Keremeos Columns one can appreciate the hardiness of the surrounding landscape. From where this picture was taken the area is arid and waterless. Only vegetation that requires very little water will grow on this semi-arid mountain slope. Conifers are spotted throughout the mountainside, but offer very little shade. The Keremeos Columns are hexagonal pillars of lava that cooled slowly about 30 million years ago. This is a long uphill trek that is worthy of your efforts. Leave early in the morning to avoid the sweltering sun. Make sure you take a plenty of water.

Title page: Many hikes throughout the Central and South Okanagan offer high vantage points with rewarding views of Okanagan Lake and the surrounding landscape.

Printed in Canada

Rocky Mountain Books acknowledges the financial support for its publishing program from the Government of Canada through the Canada Book Fund (CBF) and the Canada Council for the Arts, and from the province of British Columbia through the British Columbia Arts Council and the Book Publishing Tax Credit.

This book was produced using FSC®-certified, acid-free paper, processed chlorine-free and printed with vegetable-based inks

Disclaimer

The actions described in this book may be considered inherently dangerous activities. Individuals undertake these activities at their own risk. The information put forth in this guide has been collected from a variety of sources and is not guaranteed to be completely accurate or reliable. Many conditions and some information may change owing to weather and numerous other factors beyond the control of the authors and publishers. Individual climbers and/or hikers must determine the risks, use their own judgment, and take full responsibility for their actions. Do not depend on any information found in this book for your own personal safety. Your safety depends on your own good judgment based on your skills, education, and experience.
    It is up to the users of this guidebook to acquire the necessary skills for safe experiences and to exercise caution in potentially hazardous areas. The authors and publishers of this guide accept no responsibility for your actions or the results that occur from another's actions, choices, or judgments. If you have any doubt as to your safety or your ability to attempt anything described in this guidebook, do not attempt it.

Introduction

About the South Okanagan Valley

Stretching north to south in south-central British Columbia, the Okanagan Valley is almost 200 kilometres long, with an average width of 20 kilometres. Lying between the Cascade and Columbia mountain ranges, the South Okanagan Valley extends from Kelowna to Osoyoos, including Peachland, Summerland, Penticton and Oliver. The valley extends well into Washington state. In this region, the Monashee Mountains are the prominent subrange of the Columbia mountain range. Known for its climate, and enjoying consequent popularity as a summer playground, the region contains lakes that are plentiful and large, characterized by an oblong shape, which is generally the result of glacial advancement and retreat.

The soil of the South Okanagan is mainly a mixture of sand, silt and gravel, resulting in fertile land for farming. With the average annual precipitation being only 345 mm, and average summer high temperatures of 27.2°C, with 304 days of sunshine, the Okanagan Valley is the richest, most diverse and productive agricultural zone in British Columbia, after the Fraser Valley. Winters are mild, and although snow can fall with ferocity, it doesn't stay for long, so spring in the lowlands of the valley arrives early. This usually allows for a relatively timely start to the hiking season.

Oliver and Osoyoos are the only true desert areas in Canada. All other regions are classified as semi-arid, with sparse forests and open grasslands. The South Okanagan has plenty of hiking and backpacking routes. There are dozens of parks and recreational areas, and just as many provincial parks, providing ample trails with incredible views. The hillsides are rolling mounds with countless ridges and modest peaks. This zone is truly a day hiker's dream.

Fruit trees are not native to the Okanagan, although they are one of the most abundant species up and down the valley. Hiram Smith planted the first fruit trees near Osoyoos in the late 1850s. Today, crops include apples, peaches, pears, plums, apricots and cherries. Indigenous forests are comprised mainly of varieties of hemlock and cedar. Intense summer heat combined with dry air readily burns off grasses on open hillsides by late June, leaving cactus and sagebrush to dominate the open hillsides.

Getting there

Highway 97 runs the length of the Okanagan Valley and can be accessed from Vancouver through the winding Crowsnest Highway (Highway 3). The Crowsnest Highway originates at Hope and divides into highways 3 and 3A at the town of Keremeos. Highway 3 reaches Highway 97 at Osoyoos, while Highway 3A intersects with Highway 97 further north at Penticton. Alternatively, take the Coquihalla Highway from Hope to Merritt, veering off the Coquihalla onto Highway 97C. This will also take you to the South Okanagan, arriving at Peachland.

From Calgary, discover the Okanagan Valley by travelling west on the Trans-Canada Highway and turning south at Sicamous onto Highway 97A. From Sicamous, much of the North Okanagan is travelled before reaching Kelowna.

Seasonal road closures

There are no planned seasonal highway closures through the Okanagan Valley, but inclement winter weather can create unscheduled temporary closures.

All gravel Forest Service Roads (FSRs) are subject to late fall, winter and early spring closures, as many of them are not maintained during these times. In the spring runoff period, many FSRs can be closed for several weeks and some can even be washed away altogether. This has never been quite as evident as it became in the spring of 2012 when several gravel and paved roads were washed out and not repaired until mid- to late summer. Refer to the provincial website www.drivebc.ca for updates.

Facilities

Kelowna, Peachland, Summerland, Penticton and Oliver all have full facilities. These include camping with full RV hookups, resorts, hotels, B&Bs and motels. Lakeside accommodation is available in all of these centres for those of you wanting to mix a little decadence with your hiking.

Weather

Summers in the South Okanagan are mild, with hot days, warm nights and low humidity. July and August weather is considered tropical, with temperatures commonly reaching the mid-30s and averaging 27.2°C, with 304 days of sunshine annually. Precipitation averages about 345 mm each year.

Winters are mild, with moderate snowfall and average temperatures hovering just above 0°C. Cold snaps as low as −25°C can last for a couple of weeks at a time, but those are rare.

What does this mean for us day hikers? Despite snowpack runoff from higher elevations into the lowland, the hiking season begins in early spring in many areas. Some trails are snow-free as early as March and April. Summer months are obviously dry and hot, but autumn provides cooler hiking conditions before the snow falls, allowing some late-season trekking.

Drinking water

Although creeks and drainage channels are abundant during spring and early summer, most secondary water sources dry up soon after snowmelt. This creates a scarcity of drinking water during the bulk of hiking season, so bring your day's water supply from home, campground or motel. Even during spring runoff, when water is plentiful, bear in mind that this is an agricultural and ranching region, so the water may not be as pure as it appears. *Giardia lamblia* is the primary parasite that contaminates these waters and it can cause a variety of symptoms including diarrhea, gas or bloating, headache, nausea and a low-grade fever. Even the large lakes contain contaminants, and levels of fecal coliform can be high during the summer months as the shoreline's cabins and resorts reach capacity.

Wildlife concerns

The two foremost wildlife concerns in the Okanagan are black bears and cougars, with bears being the more common of the two. Stay alert for bears at all times; there could be one around any corner. Make noise, travel in groups and keep a sharp eye on the trail. Bears come out of hibernation in early spring, looking to fill their empty bellies with as many berries as they can find, so as you enter a clearing or an avalanche slope, look first before going in. The best way to avoid a bear encounter is to avoid a bear encounter. Get out of their way!

Small wildlife can also be bothersome. The hot, dry Okanagan climate is ideal for ticks, and spring is when they are at their peak. Generally, their lifecycle makes them a danger during April, May and June, but the tick season can occur later if spring has been excessively wet. Most ticks in the Okanagan are wood ticks and do not carry Lyme disease bacteria. Check your clothing before getting into your vehicle after a hike so you don't take any of the little critters back home with you. And don't forget to check family pets if they've been out hiking with you.

Safety tips

Carry bear spray with you at all times, even on short hikes. Bears in the Okanagan are becoming more urbanized as humans encroach on their territory, so they may be closer to a roadside stroll than you might think. It is always a good idea to travel in groups to deter curious bears and for assistance if someone should become injured or ill.

Stay on the trails. Many of the trails and FSRs in this area skirt cliffs and ledges that have substantial drops. As well, getting caught up in gnarly rocks or windfallen trees can easily result in a twisted ankle.

There is good cellular coverage throughout most of the hikes in this guide, so carrying a cell phone is good for emergencies or to ease the minds of loved ones awaiting your return should you run late. Although registration with park authorities or the RCMP is not necessary for any of the trails in this guide, you should always let someone know where you are going and when you expect to return, even if you are travelling in a group. An entire group can be in danger and out of cell range just as easily as an individual hiker.

Take a small flashlight with you in case you return after sunset. No matter how well you plan your hike, there are always unforeseen events that can keep you after dark.

Keep your dog on a leash. If your pet encounters a bear, he will bark and chase it around long enough to put the bear into frenzy, and when this frenzy becomes too much for your dog to handle, he's going to come back to you, and guess who's going to follow him. Yes, the angry bear.

The Okanagan has regular hunting seasons in the fall (even a few minor migratory bird seasons in the summer), so wear brightly coloured clothing from mid-September onward. A bright orange hat is also a good idea in the fall. Check the Region 8 British Columbia Hunting & Trapping Regulations Synopsis for open areas before heading out (www.env.gov. bc.ca/fw/wildlife/hunting/regulations).

Sensational vistas are seen from Okanagan Mountain Provincial Park, including these of Okanagan Lake from the North Viewpoint.

Using this Book

How the trails were chosen

This book describes day hikes throughout the South Okanagan Valley. Digging deeper into each region, the Kelowna section refers to treks around Kelowna, West Kelowna and Westside Road. Other regions include Penticton, Naramata, Oliver, Osoyoos, Summerland, Peachland and Keremeos.

I have selected the most scenic and interesting trails in these entire regions. Some are riverside strolls, some are walks to the tops of mountains, some will take you into the guts of canyons and some others will show you some marvellous meadows. I have been hiking throughout the South Okanagan and Shuswap for many years and have made certain that I have selected only the best trails out of the extensive number to choose from.

My motivation for composing this book, as well as my *Aspiring Hiker's Guide* series, is simple: I love to see people out on the trail. I like to encourage people to put on their boots and get out and hike. So this book, and others that I write, are intended to encourage everyone to get off the couch and get outside and enjoy the beauty that is waiting at their doorstep.

Trails

Many of the hikes in this book have unmarked trailheads, so I have worked painstakingly hard to ensure that the directions to trailheads are accurate. Blue Grouse Mountain, Carrot Mountain Bluffs, Keremeos Columns and Mount Boucherie are only a few of the many trails that do not have trailhead markers.

On the other end of the spectrum, treks such as Rose Valley Regional Park, Angel Springs, Mill Creek, Bear Creek Canyon Rim, Lost Lake and the Knox Mountain trails all have well-marked trailheads. One common theme that seems to characterize most of the network of trails is that forks in the paths are generally not marked. Therefore, if my directions seem to go a bit overboard, that is the reason why. I don't want you to waste countless hours going in circles, unable to find the destination. Please pay close attention to the directions and you will have a magnificent day.

Numbered text

For ease of use and simplicity, each trek's routes have been broken down into numbered paragraphs to enable a smoother flow of direction.

Difficulty

These are day hikes, but there is significant variation from route to route. Some are all but level, while others are nothing short of a straight skyward climb. Consequently, there is a basic grading system ranging from easy to strenuous. The difficulty of trails is decided on three factors: grade, distance and potential exposure to dangerous terrain.

Distances and definitions

All distances are quoted from the trailhead to the destination and back, as round-trip hikes. Should a particular route have the option of becoming a "Through" hike (see #1 just below), split the round-trip hike's distance in half to obtain the through distance. "Loop" hikes (#2 below) are measured from the trailhead as a single route that arcs around and returns to the trailhead.

Height gain (where relevant) and a rough estimate of the time needed to complete a round trip are included in the header for each route. The elevation of each route's highest point is also noted.

There are three categories of hikes, with some being a combination of two categories:

1. Through: These are routes that have a parking lot at each end. All Through hikes can become Return hikes, of course, if you have not arranged to have

a second vehicle waiting at the far end and you instead just retrace your steps to return to your starting point.

2. Loop: These hikes complete a circuit, beginning and ending at the same point but not retracing your steps. Some Loop hikes will have an additional "sub-loop" somewhere along their route that departs from and ultimately returns to the original Loop trail.

3. Return: These hikes are usually associated with mountain summit destinations. There is only one way in and the same way back out.

Sketch maps

Trails are sketched as a succession of green dots that are highlighted with a yellow glow. Main roads and highways appear as continuous yellow lines, while secondary roads, including gravel FSRs, are represented by solid red lines. Where a trailhead begins within a parking lot, a green and white parking lot symbol identifies the trailhead. Where there are no parking lots, such as a roadside pullover, or where the trailhead is some way from a parking lot, then a hiker symbol is used to designate the trailhead. The maps are to scale but are not detailed. The combination of map and written direction will easily guide you to each trailhead and its destination.

Other maps

Canadian Topographical Maps can be used should you require more detail. Natural Resources Canada topographic classification maps referenced for the South Okanagan are 82 E/3, 82 E/4, 82 E/5, 82 E/6, 82 E/11, 82 E/12, 82 E/13 and 82 E/14.

What to wear

Dress for the heat and direct sunlight in June, July and August. Temperatures readily reach, and exceed, 35°C in the summer months, and with long days, heat stroke is an ever-present danger. A hat and sunscreen are also highly recommended. Short pants and a wickable, short-sleeved shirt will help keep you cool as well. Although the weather can change, it is not usually abrupt, but packing a light jacket or raingear is a good idea. Mosquito repellent also will help make your hiking trips much more enjoyable.

As the summer fades, the days become shorter and cooler, so dress accordingly. A heavier jacket and long pants will be more comfortable during cool autumn day hikes. Spring hiking can be damp as well as cold, so raingear is also recommended.

Light hiking boots will suffice for all routes in this book.

These wonderful vineyards at Covert Farms are passed along the way to McIntyre Bluff. Beauty such as this is seen throughout the South Okanagan Valley.

Area Map

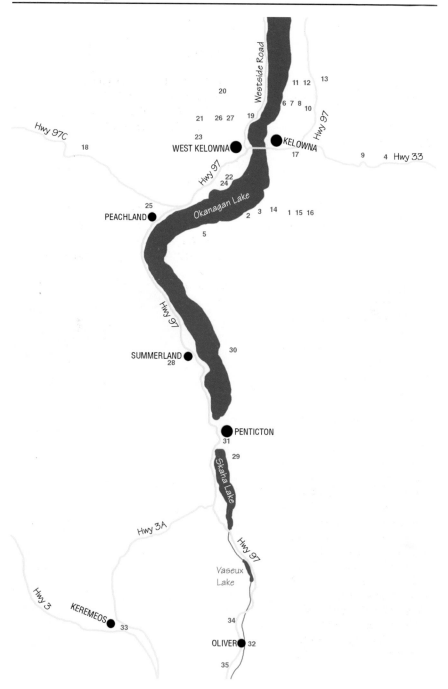

The Trails

1. Angel Springs

Category: Return
Distance: 7.6 km round trip
Height gain: 137 m
High point: 1065 m
Time: 2.5–3.5 hrs. round trip
Difficulty: Moderate
Seasons: Spring, summer, fall
Trailhead coordinates: N49 48.485
   W119 22.505

Directions to trailhead: The Angel Springs Trail is situated in the northeast corner of Myra-Bellevue Provincial Park. In Kelowna, from the intersection of Highway 97 and Gordon Dr., travel south on Gordon for 2 km to K.L.O. Rd. Turn left on K.L.O. Rd. and drive 3.9 km to McCulloch Rd. Turn right onto McCulloch Rd. Keep to McCulloch Rd. for 3.1 km, paying close attention to street markers, as McCulloch has a couple of 80–90° curves that can easily be missed. Turn right onto June Springs Rd. This road winds through southeast Kelowna for roughly 6 km until it ends at a gravel Forest Service Road. The trailhead parking lot is 1.1 km up the Little White Forest Service Road.

This is an interesting hike comprised of mixed forest and a variety of undergrowth. The calcite mineral tufa deposits created by the springs are a unique Okanagan feature, making this an extraordinary experience. Keep in mind that the springs are not hot, or even warm, in the spring and early summer as winter runoff mixes with the spring water, cooling it as it arrives at the surface. The trail beyond the official end of the trail is not well maintained, so please be careful and use at your own risk.

1. The trailhead is across the road and 60 m up the road from the parking lot. The trail goes directly into a forest of pine and cedar. This is a single-track trail with noticeably lush undergrowth.

2. The trail climbs almost imperceptibly for the first 20 to 25 minutes before flattening out, but before it does level out (about ten minutes from the trailhead) a sign directs you left.

3. You will come across two additional minor forks after the path flattens, but the way is obvious: go left both times. At the 1.3-km mark, one signed junction bears particular attention, as going straight will put you on the Myra Canyon Bailout Trail, sending you on an entirely different journey.

4. This is an interpretive trail, so there are informative signs suitably placed throughout the trek, describing tree species, seasonal wetlands, Okanagan hotspots and faults, among other interesting topics.

5. A tranquil marsh is tucked away behind the forest on your left, just past the Myra Canyon Bailout junction. As the interpretive sign suggests, this is a "seasonal" wetland, so it will be either a marsh or a meadow, depending on the time of year and the heat of the summer sun.

6. About an hour, or three kilometres, from the trailhead, you will begin an 83 m downhill trek to the springs. The vegetation changes abruptly to become dark, canopied forest comprised mainly of western red cedar. Here the springs filter down from the slopes above, becoming braided as they travel over the forest floor.

7. There is room for exploration beyond the initial encounter with the springs, but these trails are makeshift and not properly maintained, so be careful and watch for damp roots on the forest floor.

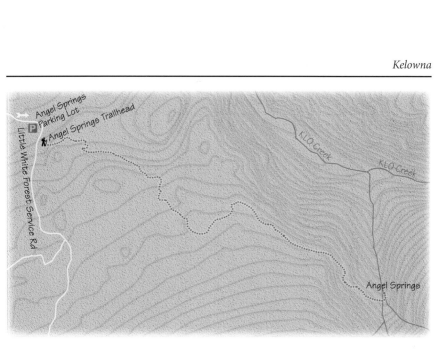

Much of the hike into Angel Springs consists of a forested walk among magnificent pine and cedar trees.

The remarkable Angel Springs is seen here mixed with spring runoff. It is not until later in the season when water levels are low that the springs can achieve any significant heat.

2. Cedar Mountain Regional Park Viewpoint

Category: Return
Distance: 2.6 km round trip
Height gain: 69 m
High point: 807 m
Time: 1–2 hrs. round trip
Difficulty: Easy
Seasons: Spring, summer, late fall
Trailhead coordinates: N49 46.444
   W119 31.287

Not many trails in this area offer such generous sights for such nominal effort as the trails in this park do. There is minimal elevation gain and very little hiking distance. The trail runs through the remains of a forest that was destroyed by fire in the summer of 2003.

Directions to trailhead: From the intersection of Highway 97 and Gordon Dr. in downtown Kelowna, drive south on Gordon for 6.7 km to DeHart Rd. Turn right on DeHart and drive for 400 m to reach Lakeshore Rd. Turn left onto Lakeshore Rd. and travel 1.5 km to a traffic-controlled intersection. Continue straight through the intersection onto what is now Chute Lake Rd. (At this intersection, Lakeshore Rd. continues as a 90° right turn.) Drive along Chute Lake Rd. for 3.2 km and turn left onto Mountainside Dr. Travel on Mountainside for 600 m until you reach Chute Lake Rd. (again), which is now a gravel road. Turn right onto Chute Lake Rd. and drive 1.6 km. The parking lot for Cedar Mountain Regional Park is on your right.

1. The trek begins as a flat walk on a dirt road, and in a couple of minutes the trail crosses Lebanon Creek on a small bridge.

2. The trail continues its reasonably flat course, gaining only 12 m of elevation for about 600 m until it intersects with a second dirt road deviating off to the right toward some rock bluffs. Take the right fork here, as these bluffs are the ultimate goal of this hike. The main road you just left carries on for only another five minutes or so, whereupon it ends at the park boundary though continuing as a private drive.

3. Watch closely now for a single-track path that leaves this road within a couple of minutes, also departing to the right. Get on this single-track trail.

4. The trail takes you down a steep face into a gully only to bring you back up a steeper rock wall on the other side. It will take you several minutes to make your way up the wall as it switchbacks its way between layers of rock.

5. The trail will plateau to open grass at the top of the rock wall, and right away you should look for another trail veering off to the left. Continuing straight presents its own rewards of scenery and is worth the tangent if you have the time.

6. By taking the left trail, your journey up to the top of the uppermost bluff is greatly assisted by 50–60 stone steps. Someone has contributed many hours of labour to provide this beautiful staircase, taking you close to the summit of the highest bluff.

7. Where the stone steps end, the voyage resumes on a soil path, still climbing but only for about five more minutes. The way to the large summit is marked with cairns.

8. Views from the summit of this flat-topped bluff are magnificent. The obvious spectacle is Okanagan Lake to the west, northwest and north, but looking behind you to the west and south, you can still view the destruction of the fires of 2003 for almost as far as you can see.

The scope of the devastation from the 2003 forest fire season can be witnessed from any highpoint on the Cedar Mountain trail.

The Cedar Mountain viewpoint offers views aside from a burnt forest. There is a clear line of sight up and down Okanagan Lake. The top view is to the north, while the bottom image is looking south.

3. Jack Smith Lake Trail

Category: Return
Distance: 5 km round trip
Height gain: 89 m
High point: 666 m
Time: 1–2 hrs. round trip
Difficulty: Easy
Seasons: Spring, summer, late fall
Trailhead coordinates: N49 47.926
    W119 28.413

Directions to trailhead: In Kelowna, at the intersection of Highway 97 and Gordon Dr., drive south on Gordon for about 10 km to South Crest Dr. Right away, South Crest Dr. veers left and becomes Clarence Ave. Follow Clarence for about 700 m to Kuipers Crescent. Turn left onto Kuipers Crescent and look for the sign for Kuipers Peak Mountain Park. The trailhead for the hike to Jack Smith Lake is shared with the trailhead for Kuipers Peak Trail. There is no parking lot; only pullover areas on the side of the road.

1. This pleasant hike begins on a wide gravel path that immediately presents sprawling views of South Kelowna and Okanagan Lake. It climbs moderately for about five minutes to reach its high point early in the hike. The remnants of the 2003 forest fires are very evident throughout this region as well – the nearby landscape is dotted with spots of green, unharmed conifers that are surrounded with less-fortunate burnt ones.

2. About a half a kilometre from the trailhead you will come across a communication tower and a water reservoir. Directly in front of the reservoir, a short, narrow path takes you to a small mound of boulders that offers fantastic scenery.

3. The main trail now blends in with the reservoir/communication tower service road and begins a gradual decline in elevation.

4. Almost immediately after leaving the reservoir, the road comes to a fork. Take the left fork travelling downward toward the valley bottom.

5. About five minutes into the descent (one kilometre into the hike), look for a sharp left turn in the road and stay on this as it travels a ridge for several hundred metres. There are numerous trails in the area, but staying on the road is the more direct route to Jack Smith Lake.

6. The lake comes into view after five to seven minutes of walking on the ridge.

7. Once you have spotted the lake, the trail begins a sharp drop down toward the bottom of the valley where it resides. You will find yourself lakeside shortly thereafter.

The tranquil Jack Smith Lake.

The gem that is Jack Smith Lake is found among the Okanagan's rapidly growing urban sprawl, some of which can be seen in these two images. This area is one of the fastest-growing regions in the province, yet there is no shortage of sensational natural scenery if you look beyond the buildings.

4. High Rim Trail (Mission Creek Loop)

Category: Loop
Distance: 3.4 km round trip
Height gain: 87 m descent
High point: 849 m
Time: 45–90 mins. round trip
Difficulty: Easy
Seasons: Early spring, summer,
     late fall
Trailhead coordinates: N49 51.851
     W119 11.456

Directions to trailhead: Drive north from downtown Kelowna on Harvey Ave. to the intersection of Harvey Ave. and Highway 33. Turn right (east) on Highway 33 and travel for 20 km, where Philpott Rd. meets Highway 33 on the left (north) side of the highway. There is a small parking lot at this junction. The trailhead is about 100 m back down Highway 33, on the south side of the road.

This is a great day hike for children, or for adult hikers who are looking for a quick, easy adventure into the woods with the pleasant company of a swift creek at a tranquil resting spot.

1. After crossing the highway, make your way over a wire fence at the side of the road. This feat is accomplished with the assistance of a couple of wooden steps on both sides of the fence. The trail begins as it enters a forest of western red cedar as a single-track path.

2. This is an easy hike, as it progresses from a gentle, downward, slopeside stroll that levels off rather quickly.

3. Ten minutes into the hike, the path widens and the sound of rushing water can be heard in the distance below you.

4. A few minutes later, a road approaches from the left of the now widened trail. Stay to the right, maintaining course toward the creek below.

5. Ten minutes later the destination is attained. This is well marked with multiple signs explaining where you are, where you can go, who built the trail and what the elevation is. One sign guides you across the creek to pick up the Okanagan Highlands Trail on the opposite bank. The trail can be spotted from this vantage point. The last time I was here was in October, so at that time of year the thought of exploring the other side of the creek was not that appealing.

6. This is a pleasant piece of the planet that allows you to sit and enjoy Mission Creek as it rushes by. There are ample grassy spaces along the bank on which to have a picnic.

7. Take the same route back, but take the left fork (now the right fork) at the previously encountered junction to complete a small loop totalling 3.4 km.

8. As you break through the forest onto the road, your vehicle will be a quick paved walk away, about 750 m to your left.

The hike to Mission Creek provides a relaxed setting and is just a short distance from the paved road.

The hike to Mission Creek along this portion of the High Rim Trail begins as a pleasant walk through shaded forest.

The destination offers grassy areas to rest comfortably as the creek rambles by.

5. Okanagan Mountain Provincial Park (North Viewpoint)

Category: Return
Distance: 5.6 km round trip
Height gain: 283 m
High point: 684 m
Time: 2–3 hrs. round trip
Difficulty: Moderate
Seasons: Spring, summer, late fall
Trailhead coordinates: N49 46.895
    W119 35.474

Directions to trailhead: From the intersection of Highway 97 and Pandosy St., drive south on Pandosy. After 2.5 km, at K.L.O. Rd., Pandosy St. becomes Lakeshore Rd. Travel along Lakeshore Rd. for 12.5 km to the Okanagan Mountain Provincial Park parking lot, on the right side of the road. This road becomes very narrow in places and is a popular cycling route, so drive with caution. The trailhead is on the opposite side of the road.

This hike takes you to one of the park's most bountiful viewpoints, providing scenery in every direction. It makes its way through a region of sparse conifers and grasslands.

1. The trail begins as an uphill, single-track path and continues to climb, with periodic flat zones. This trek takes you through what was once a flourishing forest that was transformed by fire to become grassland with burnt, defoliated red cedar and western hemlock.

2. Fifteen minutes from the trailhead, the path begins to give up much of the elevation that was gained, by heading down to a gully that has a beautiful creek running through it. This stream is called Deeper Creek.

Charred remnants of a once lively forest remain throughout this region of Okanagan Mountain Provincial Park.

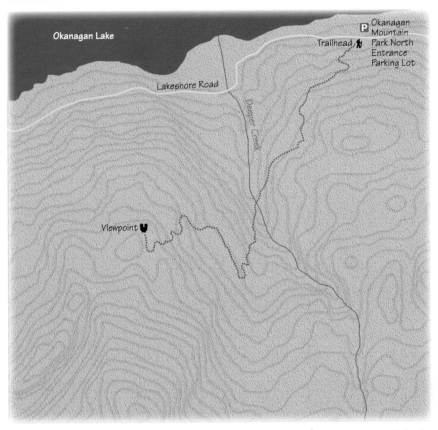

3. You will cross Deeper Creek via a short wooden bridge about 1.3 km into the hike. Of course, once you're at the bottom of the gully, you must come back up out of it, so you will commence climbing as soon as you cross the creek.

4. The climb continues for another 10–15 minutes, whereupon it engages a significant intersection at the 1.8-km mark of the journey (35–40 minutes).

5. You have the option of continuing straight to get to Divide Lake or turning right, up to the viewpoint that is our destination, so turn right onto Wild Horse Canyon Trail.

6. For the next kilometre, the trail climbs at a steady, yet moderate pace until it meets up with signs directing you upward to the viewpoint on the right. This is hard to miss, as one sign says "Scenic Route," while the other indicates the viewpoint is to the right.

7. A short uphill push brings you to a large flat piece of land that supplies scenes of Okanagan Lake and the town of Peachland. Behind you, looking south and east, the view consists of a mixture of dead, charred trees (standing and fallen), as well as some firs that survived the 2003 fires.

Okanagan Lake looking north from Okanagan Mountain Provincial Park's north viewpoint.

The town of Peachland, on the western shore of Okanagan Lake, is plainly seen from the Okanagan Mountain Provincial Park's north viewpoint on a clear day.

6. Knox Mountain Park – Apex Lookout

Category: Return
Distance: 4.4 km round trip
Height gain: 271 m
High point: 623 m
Time: 1–2 hrs. round trip
Difficulty: Moderately strenuous
Seasons: Spring, summer, fall
Trailhead coordinates: N49 54.326
   W119 29.453

Directions to trailhead: From Harvey Ave. in Kelowna, turn north onto Ellis St. Drive to the end of Ellis, to the Knox Mountain Park lower parking lot. Ellis St. continues past the far end of the parking lot as a paved park road, arriving at two more parking lots farther up. The first upper parking lot eliminates some of the trail's elevation and distance, but the explanation below begins at the lower parking lot. Regardless, there is a gate that disallows vehicular traffic and it is closed most of the time.

This trail, in the heart of Kelowna, provides a terrific cardiovascular workout while offering splendid views from the summit.

1. The trail begins as a gravel path heading up the left side of the above-mentioned paved road. This trail is well defined, as it is heavily used.

2. Continue upward, tracking a fenceline that accompanies the trail. Following directional signs, you will come within ten minutes to a staircase constructed of landscaping ties. There are about 80 steps to climb.

3. The trail reaches the upper parking lot a few minutes beyond the top of the stairs. The trail picks up at the far right (north) end of the upper parking lot. You have now walked 700 m and gained 92 m in elevation.

4. As you leave the parking lot onto the trail, take the ascending trail on your right. This will eventually reach the Apex summit.

5. For the next 20–30 minutes, the trail winds steadily upward. This continuous climb is interrupted by a couple of forks in the trail, but on both occasions, the split trails reunite to form a single path.

6. The last few minutes to the lookout are gratefully made easier with a wooden staircase of close to 100 steps.

7. The lookout is a wooden, gazebo-like structure with a metal roof, which accommodates about twenty people quite comfortably. Although the shelter provides 360° vistas, looking to the west and south offers a bigger bounty for the eyes, with Okanagan Lake, West Kelowna, Kelowna, Glenmore and the William R. Bennett Bridge in the spotlight.

8. Return the same way.

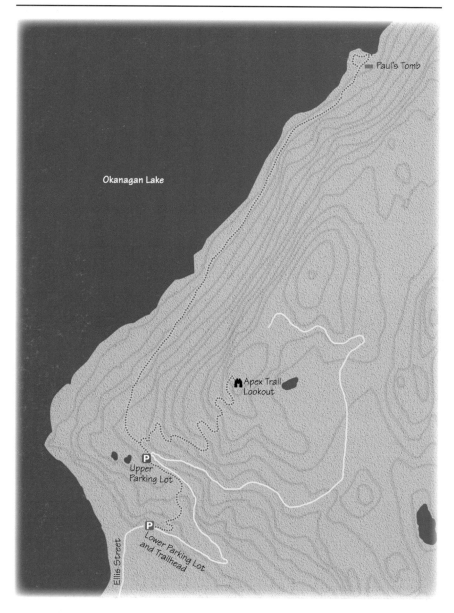

Views from Knox Mountain Park – Apex Lookout. A stunning panorama of Okanagan Lake looking to the north.

Downtown Kelowna with Okanagan Lake in the backdrop viewed from Knox Mountain Park – Apex Lookout.

7. Knox Mountain Park – Paul's Tomb

Category: Return
Distance: 6.8 km round trip
Height gain: 92 m
High point: 446 m
Time: 1–2 hrs. round trip
Difficulty: Moderate
Seasons: Spring, summer, fall
Trailhead coordinates: N49 54.326
    W119 29.453

Directions to trailhead: From Harvey Ave. in Kelowna, turn north onto Ellis St. Drive to the end of Ellis to the Knox Mountain Park lower parking lot. Ellis St. continues past the far end of the parking lot as a paved park road, arriving at two more parking lots farther up. The first upper parking lot eliminates some of the trail's elevation and distance, but the explanation below begins at the lower parking lot. Regardless, there is a gate that disallows vehicular traffic and it is closed most of the time.

The first part of this trek is an uphill climb, but beyond that it is a pleasant, effortless stroll alongside Okanagan Lake. The goal of the hike is to reach the tomb of Rembler Paul and his wife, Elizabeth. Rembler Paul was born in Montreal in 1932. While his occupation was as a veterinary surgeon, he yearned to travel west and north. He later became a successful, wealthy real estate and mining entrepreneur in Regina, Saskatchewan, and eventually settled in Kelowna in 1905, where he and Elizabeth lived in a large house on Bernard Ave. Wanting to leave a legacy for both himself and his wife, Paul had the tomb built in 1910. Rembler Paul died in 1916, two years after his wife.

See map on page 30.

1. The trail begins as a gravel path heading up the left side of the above-mentioned paved road. This trail is well defined, as it is heavily used.

2. Continue upward, tracking a fenceline that accompanies the trail. Following directional signs, you will come to a staircase constructed of landscaping ties within ten minutes. There are about 80 steps in this staircase.

3. The trail reaches the upper parking lot a few minutes beyond the top of the stairs. The trail picks up at the far right (north) end of the upper parking lot. You have now walked 700 m and gained 92 m in elevation.

4. As you leave the parking lot onto the trail, the trail splits. Stay on the main trail travelling straight.

5. The wide gravel path remains flat for almost half a kilometre before it eventually begins to descend to the shoreline of Okanagan Lake.

6. The journey is an uninterrupted downhill meander, with only one exception: where a side trail joins the main trail, there is a marker informing you there is one kilometre remaining.

7. The destination, the tomb of Rembler Paul and his wife, Elizabeth, is almost at water level. There is some disappointment at the final goal, as the entrance to the tomb has been filled in with soil and capped with concrete to prevent grave-robbing. All that remains visible is the year "D1910" etched into the concrete. The tomb is on the right (east) side of the trail as you approach the end of the trail. This area is also a fantastic picnic spot, complete with tables, lawn, outhouses and a wonderful little swimming bay.

*A spectacular sunny view looking north up
Okanagan Lake along the trail to Paul's Tomb.*

*The destination of the Knox Mountain Park
Paul's Tomb trek offers a splendid beach
with a wonderful swimming area.*

8. Knox Mountain Park – Kathleen Lake

Category: Return with an end loop
Distance: 7 km round trip
Height gain: 180 m
High point: 534 m
Time: 2–3 hrs. round trip
Difficulty: Moderate
Seasons: Spring, summer, fall
Trailhead coordinates: N49 54.326
   W119 29.453

Directions to trailhead: From Harvey Ave. in Kelowna, turn north onto Ellis St. Drive to the end of Ellis St. to the Knox Mountain Park lower parking lot. Ellis St. continues past the far end of the parking lot as a paved park road, arriving at two upper parking lots farther up. The first upper parking lot eliminates some of the trail's elevation and distance, but the explanation below begins at the lower parking lot. Regardless, there is a gate that disallows vehicular traffic and it is closed most of the time.

Most of this hike is accomplished on paved road, but there is an alternative route that uses a trail instead of the paved road to get to the first upper parking lot. Refer to either Knox Mountain Park – Paul's Tomb (#7) or Knox Mountain Park – Apex Lookout (#6) for the alternative route. The all-road option was chosen to the Kathleen Lake turnoff because directions were vague at the time of writing and I did not want to overshoot it. So this trek uses the all-road route.

1. Make your way up the busy park road for a little over a kilometre, arriving at the first of the two upper parking lots in about 20 minutes.

2. Continuing up the main road brings you to a viewing bench about ten minutes from the first parking lot.

This is a tranquil spot within a very busy park. Take your time to explore the area around you as you complete a loop around the lake.

3. Five minutes later you will see the Kathleen Lake Trail turnoff sign, with the trail on your right. You are 2.5 km from the trailhead.

4. The way is evident as the dirt road you are on immediately goes straight across a couple of minor intersecting trails.

5. Three to five minutes from the Kathleen Lake Trail turnoff, a sign directing you to the right comes into view. This is the beginning of the loop around the lake.

6. This is not really a lakeside stroll, since the forested trail is considerably high as it loops around the lake. However, there are side trails that take you down to the lake farther into the hike.

7. At the far end of the lake, you come to a high retaining wall that is close to a residential property. Turn left, as the road becomes a narrow, single-track path.

8. After a couple of minutes up a slight rise, you will exit the forest and enter a large meadow where the trail meets a gravel road. Turn left onto the road.

9. This road parallels the east side of the lake, high above it, but there are a couple of trails that take you down to the shoreline.

10. There is a point where the trail reaches a four-way intersection. The sign to complete the loop will send you to the left.

11. A few minutes later you will complete the loop. Turn right to return to the main road.

The well-marked entrance to Kathleen Lake as it departs the paved road.

Glimpses of Kathleen Lake are seen through the forest as the trail makes its way around the entire perimeter of the lake.

The north end of Kathleen Lake allows close access to its shoreline.

9. Black Knight Mountain

Category: Return
Distance: 12 km round trip
Height gain: 513 m
High point: 1274 m
Time: 3–4 hrs. round trip
Difficulty: Moderately strenuous
Seasons: Late spring, summer, early fall
Trailhead coordinates: N49 51.749 W119 18.444

Don't let all the "Private Property" and "Unauthorized Access Not Permitted" signs turn you away from this magnificent hike. The owner permits hikers on this road, as long as they stick to the road, and farther up the trail a marker indicates where Crown land begins. Crown land grants the public use of this property. This is an uphill hike from beginning to end.

Directions to trailhead: At the north end of Kelowna, at the junction of Highway 97 and Highway 33, travel east on 33 toward Rutland. Drive for 9.7 km to Pyman Rd. on the left (north side) of the highway. This is a gravel road. Park anywhere before the gate, since you will run the risk of being locked on the other side of the gate if you park beyond it. There are gravel pits in the area, so be on the lookout for truck traffic while you are hiking this route. The entire trek takes place on this gravel road.

1. This is a rather straightforward excursion, but there are a few key intersections that must be interpreted correctly or you will find yourself in a gravel pit. The first notable intersection is within the first five minutes of the hike. Here there is a fork that veers off to the left, but you want to carry on along the main road going up to the right.

2. You can see the trek's goal when you glimpse the communication towers upward to the left, so I'll state the obvious – this is a steady uphill climb. However, since the communication towers require year-round access, the road is not as steep as you might think. Regardless, continue upward as the road cuts through beautiful grasslands filled with dazzling wildflowers.

3. About 20–25 minutes, or 1.5 km, into the hike, the second notable fork in the road comes into play. Just before the main road crests, a minor road deviates to the left. Get on this left road and continue to wind your way through open grasslands. The grasslands gradually give way to a diverse forest of deciduous and coniferous species.

4. You will come to another intersection at the 3-km mark of the hike (45–50 minutes). There is a small pond at this point that is usually covered with algae, but it is also home to a couple of varieties of water lilies. Take the left fork at this junction.

5. You will meet up with a metal gate with a well-displayed "No Trespassing" sign roughly ten minutes from the pond. Disregard this sign, as you are now on Crown land, and skirt around the gate to continue to the summit.

6. The remaining half-hour of the trek (about 2 km) is an uneventful, moderate, steady, uphill climb to the summit.

7. Once you are at the summit, a glut of viewing is presented – Okanagan Lake steals the show to the west, while the Interior Plateau encompasses the scenery to the north and east. Even in early summer, snow can be seen on the far-off peaks to the south.

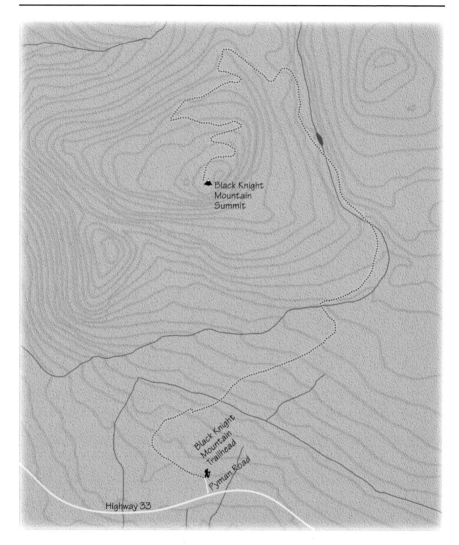

Black Knight
Mountain
Summit

Black Knight
Mountain
Trailhead

Pyman Road

Highway 33

A sea of yellow wildflowers makes the
exhausting uphill trek to the summit of Black
Knight Mountain somewhat easier. This is
one of the many rewards on this adventure.

The fields of flowers on the Black
Knight Mountain trek offer colours
other than just yellow.

The panorama from the summit of Black Knight Mountain is unparalleled. This view to the south includes not only Okanagan Lake but many of the hills that surround it.

This southward view, also from the summit, shows just how calm the large Okanagan Lake can be on a hot, sunny day.

Snow persists on the mountains in June, as seen from the summit of Black Knight Mountain looking to the east.

One of many encounters on the Black Knight Mountain trek. Although the water from this pond is not potable, simply sitting beside it offers a mild respite on a hot summer day.

10. Mount Baldy

Category: Return with an end loop
Distance: 3 km round trip
Height gain: 89 m
High point: 541 m
Time: 45–90 mins. round trip
Difficulty: Easy
Seasons: Early spring, summer,
   late fall
Trailhead coordinates: N49 54.274
   W119 25.360

Directions to trailhead: In Kelowna, at the intersection of Highway 97 and Dilworth Rd., drive north on Dilworth for 3 km. Along the way, Dilworth Rd. eventually becomes Rifle Rd. On the right side of Rifle Rd., look for a dirt road that leaves the pavement at an iron gate at the 3-km mark. There is room for only one vehicle on the dirt road before the iron gate, but parking on the street is permitted.

This short hike takes you to the top of a mountain that has now become surrounded by urban sprawl. As parkland, though, it has been left to its own destiny, so please avoid the many shortcut paths and help to preserve this natural beauty.

1. Although the ensuing directions are rather meticulous, to ensure you arrive at the summit and don't spend the day wandering the multitude of trails in this park, understand that you are simply guiding yourself toward the obvious summit that is right in front of you. Most of this trek is in an open meadow with a few diversions into some sparse forests.

2. As soon as you navigate past the iron gate, cross the first fork in the single-track trail by continuing straight.

3. A few brief minutes into the hike places you at another fork in the trail; turn left onto an old road that begins an uphill climb. The road soon becomes a path.

4. A couple of minutes later you will arrive at yet another fork in the trail. Take the right-hand trail into some trees and you will quickly intersect another track that comes at you from the right. At this point, go left. The climb to the summit begins

here as the path becomes a double-track former road again.

5. The double track splits about five minutes later – make sure you take the right fork.

6. The next fork in the path is a couple of minutes away. If you turn right onto this road, it will take you to the summit of Mount Baldy.

7. Four to six minutes of upward slogging brings you to a fantastic ridge walk. To your left you will see a beacon on the summit of the hill farthest to the northeast. You will arrive at this beacon after a 6–8 minute stroll along the grassy ridgeline.

8. From the summit, beautiful views of Mount Dilworth and the Dilworth agricultural area are prevalent, along with some vistas of Rutland. However, one of the best sights is right beneath you as you wander through gorgeous grassy slopes.

9. You can head back down the same way, or you can extend this trek by making a bit of a loop on the way back. To take the loop, head back down the ridge the same way you came and take the first right path at the first fork you come to.

10. A couple of minutes later, turn right onto a faint trail at another intersection.

11. Follow this trail for about five minutes, at which point you will come to a T-junction. Take the left fork here. You are now on a slope sidewalk through a forest of pine and spruce.

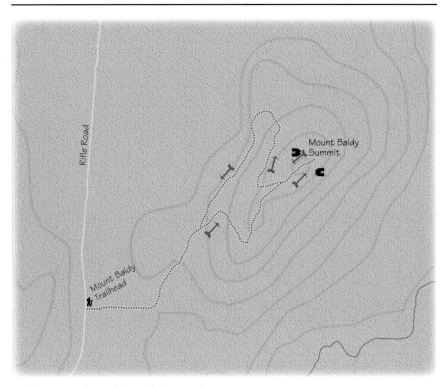

12. Carry on along this trail for another seven to eight minutes and go straight across a well-travelled intersection. This intersection completes the loop. Arriving back at your vehicle from here should take about seven to eight minutes.

The open grassy slopes of Mount Baldy
provide no relief from the sun.

Scenery is not obstructed on the slopes of Mount Baldy, and many of the local farms and vineyards are easily identified.

11. Stephens Coyote Ridge Regional Park – Ridge Walk

Category: Loop
Distance: 3.7 km
Height gain: 190 m
High point: 647 m
Time: 1–2 hrs. round trip
Difficulty: Easy
Seasons: Early spring, summer,
   late fall
Trailhead coordinates: N49 57.783
   W119 25.475

Directions to trailhead: Heading north from downtown Kelowna on Highway 97, turn left on Glenmore Rd. Drive for 9.3 km to reach the North Glenmore dog park on the left side of the road. The entrance to Stephens Coyote Ridge Regional Park is on the right (north) side of the parking lot.

This effortless loop hike presents superb views of McKinley Reservoir, Lightblue Lake, Okanagan Lake and North Glenmore, as well as Kelowna off in the distance to the south.

1. From the parking lot, get onto the wide, grassy path on the right (north) side that travels between fences on either side of the trail. This will take you into a forest within a couple of minutes.

2. Five to ten minutes later this double-wide trail comes to a meadow that presents spectacular vistas of the local countryside.

3. Wandering through this meadow for five minutes brings you to a T-junction.

Lush hillsides are part of the fun on the Stephens Coyote Ridge Regional Park ridge walk.

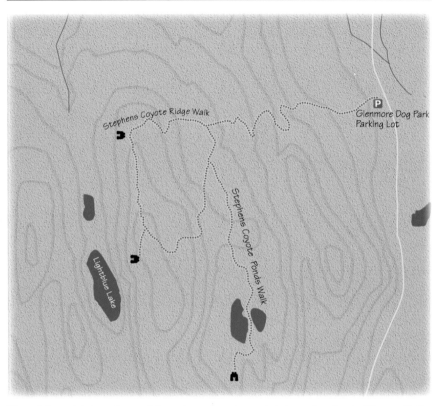

Turn right at this junction and then almost immediately take the first left down into a gully.

4. Around 15 minutes of hiking, and 85 m of elevation gain, from the T-junction brings you to the high point of this short, yet beautiful trek. There are a couple of minor trails that connect with the main route, but maintaining the correct course will be obvious. As the trail meanders toward the high point, the blue waters of the McKinley Reservoir are easily spotted on your right, as is the much smaller Lightblue Lake. Lightblue Lake becomes more visible if you take the short detour on a faint path that departs from the high point of this trek. This unmarked

viewpoint is only about 85 m off the main trail.

5. As you leave the high point, the trail begins its descent, giving back the elevation that was previously gained.

6. There are three main forks in the trail within the next 10–15 minutes, completing a loop back to the T-junction. Take the left fork at the first two junctures, and the right fork at the third. The third fork appears immediately after the second one.

7. Take a quick dip in and out of a very small gully and you will return to the T-junction in just over 100 m.

8. Turn right and make your way back to the parking lot.

A well-defined trail takes you around the perimeter of the Stephens Coyote Ridge Regional Park ridge walk.

The openness of Stephens Coyote Ridge Regional Park extends beautiful viewing in almost all directions.

12. Stephens Coyote Ridge Regional Park – Ponds Walk

Category: Return
Distance: 4 km
Height gain: 122 m
High point: 579 m
Time: 1–2 hrs. round trip
Difficulty: Easy
Seasons: Early spring, summer, late fall
Trailhead coordinates: N49 57.783 W119 25.475

Directions to trailhead: Heading north from downtown Kelowna on Highway 97, turn left on Glenmore Rd. Drive 9.3 km to reach the North Glenmore Dog Park on the left side of the road. The entrance to Stephens Coyote Ridge Regional Park is on the right (north) side of the parking lot.

See map on page 47.

This casual hike goes between two small, marshy ponds, with an abundance of waterfowl, on its way to a viewpoint that provides vistas of North Glenmore and Kelowna.

1. From the parking lot, get onto the wide grassy path on the right (north) side that travels between fences on either side of the trail. This trail will take you into a forest within a couple of minutes.

2. Five to ten minutes later this double-wide trail comes to a meadow that presents spectacular vistas of the local countryside.

3. Wandering through this meadow for five minutes brings you to a T-junction. Turn left.

The first of two gorgeous small ponds comes into view on the Stephens Coyote Ridge Regional Park ponds walk.

4. Without veering off onto any of the side trails, you will drop into and come out of a small gully 80 m from the T-junction. Seventy metres past the gully is the only key intersection in the journey. Take the left fork at this intersection.

5. Half a kilometre from the T-junction, the trail meanders up to a knoll, where suddenly the larger of the two ponds is seen.

6. The trail drops sharply down toward the plateau that encompasses the ponds, which are about 300 m from the top of the knoll.

7. Passing between the ponds, continue beyond them for another 350 m to reach a viewpoint offering sights of northern Kelowna.

8. The area beyond this viewpoint is scattered with "No Trespassing" signs, but the landowner has no problem with hikers going beyond the signs to catch a view. He has asked me to ensure that everyone cleans up after themselves, so please do.

The hike to the ponds in Stephens Coyote Regional Park are worth the effort, as many species of waterfowl and marsh-dwelling animals make this their home.

13. Mill Creek Regional Park

Category: Return
Distance: 2.6 km round trip
Height gain: 71 m
High point: 526 m
Time: 1 hr.
Difficulty: Easy
Seasons: Early spring, summer,
   late fall
Trailhead coordinates: N49 58.332
   W119 21.799

Directions to trailhead: From Quail Ridge Blvd., at the Kelowna International Airport traffic lights, travel north for 2 km to reach Old Vernon Rd. After 1.1 km, Old Vernon Rd. becomes Spencer Rd. at a yield sign. Continue along Spencer for 400 m and turn right at the "Mill Creek Recreation Area" sign. Drive a short distance to the parking lot.

This short hike begins as a streamside stroll through a cedar-shaded canyon. This shade provides refreshing relief from the blazing Okanagan summer sun.

1. The Mill Creek Trail begins as a wide path that eventually narrows to a single-track trail as the canyon becomes tighter, thus bringing the trail and creek closer together.

2. Right away the route splits into two distinct trails, but both forks quickly rejoin to create the main trail. Going left takes you on a five-minute journey up a staircase and back down again to a boardwalk, while taking the right-hand option means you will stay level, making your way through the cedar forest.

3. Shortly after the two trails become one, the route crosses Mill Creek on a sturdy, wood-beam bridge, placing the creek on the right side of the trail.

4. Five minutes past the bridge crossing, there is a small, yet noteworthy waterfall on your right. Just past this waterfall the trail begins to narrow to become a single-track path.

5. After the trail narrows, it takes two distinctive courses. Depending on the water level, you can take the high ground as it travels somewhat erratically between trees and over roots, or you can take the flatter, quicker streamside option if the water is low enough.

6. Roughly 20–25 minutes from the starting point, the second, and higher, of the two waterfalls is found. Since this is such a short hike, take some time to stop and enjoy this peaceful spot. It is very calm, beautiful and relaxing.

7. A few short minutes beyond this waterfall, you will reach the park boundary sign. Although the trail continues past the boundary, it is not maintained and becomes considerably rougher and more unpredictable.

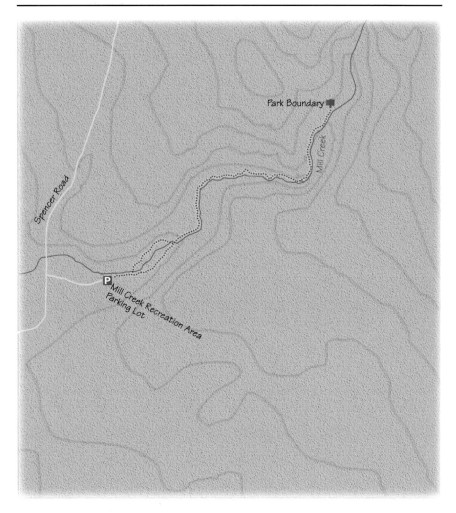

The beautiful woodlands surrounding Mill Creek make this hike most enjoyable.

The serene charm of Mill Creek is ever present on this hike.

*One of two waterfalls found
on the Mill Creek hike.*

*An "aerial" view of one of the waterfalls
encountered on the Mill Creek hike.*

14. Canyon Falls

Category: Return
Distance: 1.4 km round trip; 1.9 km
    including upper trail
Height gain: −133 m
High point: 622 m
Time: 20–30 min. round trip
Difficulty: Easy
Seasons: Spring, summer, late fall
Trailhead coordinates: N49 48.282
    W119 27.104

Directions to trailhead: In Kelowna, at the intersection of Highway 97 and Gordon Dr., drive south on Gordon for 3.7 km to Casorso Rd. Turn left on Casorso. At the second of two round-abouts get onto Swamp Rd. Go down Swamp Rd. for 2.1 km, and turn left onto DeHart Rd. About 750 m later, turn right onto Crawford Rd. Drive along Crawford for 1.5 km and turn right onto Westridge Dr. Turn right onto Canyon Ridge Dr. 1.7 km later, and then almost immediately turn right onto Canyon Falls Ct. You can park on the right side of the road.

1. The trailhead begins as a flat gravel path, but this is short-lived, as a sign at a fork in the path will point you down the canyon slope right away.

2. Except for a couple of flat spots along the way, the remainder of the hike is downhill to the canyon bottom.

This short, steep hike to Bellevue Creek falls confirms that beauty can be only moments away from your car, if you're looking for it.

3. At the time of writing, one section of eroded bank had been augmented with an aluminum ladder, making the last 10–15 m to the canyon floor a little easier.

4. The waterfalls are off to the left (south), once you are in the canyon. There is much more exploring to do other than the falls. There is a swimming hole to the right (north) and some gravel islands for sunbathing.

5. The Bellevue Creek falls are active year round. I have been here at the end of a long, dry summer, and an abundance of water was still flowing.

6. Return the same way, trying to stay on the designated trails. This area has become damaged from erratic hiking which has caused some serious erosion to the natural ecosystem on the canyon walls.

7. Once you are back up top, take the straight branch of the trail at the previously mentioned intersection instead of going down the canyon slope. This provides fantastic scenery, including sagebrush hills and glimpses into the canyon and creek as well as Okanagan Lake.

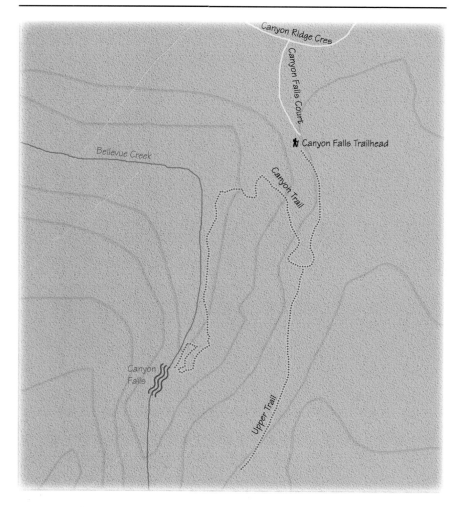

Bellevue Creek canyon from the Canyon Falls viewpoint.

This secured aluminum ladder makes it easy to get in and out of the canyon. It also adds to the excitement of adventuring in the canyon floor. The ladder was placed here to reduce the erosion that hiking on this trail was creating.

Bellevue Creek canyon with the creek in view.

Bellevue Creek downstream from the waterfalls.

One of the hazards on the way to Canyon Falls is a field of rubble. One can easily twist an ankle, so watch your step.

This is what you came for – the picturesque Canyon Falls.

15. Lost Lake Trail – Pink Highway Loop

Category: Loop
Distance: 7.5 km round trip
Height gain: 236 m
High point: 760 m
Time: 1.5–2.5 hrs. round trip
Difficulty: Easy
Seasons: Early spring, summer,
  late fall
Trailhead coordinates: N49 48.738
  W119 26.558

Directions to trailhead: In Kelowna, at the intersection of Gordon Dr. and Highway 97, drive south on Gordon for 3.7 km to Casorso Rd. Turn left onto Casorso Rd. Follow Casorso for 2.3 km as it goes through two traffic circles. At 2.3 km, the road splits into DeHart Rd. going right and Bedford Rd. going left – get onto Bedford Rd. Stay on Bedford for 1.4 km to where it intersects with Saucier Rd. and Stewart Rd. E. At this junction, Bedford Rd. terminates, so go straight onto Stewart Rd. E. After 1.5 km, Stewart Rd E. ends at the Myra-Bellevue Provincial Park parking lot.

Due to a fire that ravaged this area in 2003, this loop hike takes you through a mixture of sparse forest with spots of dense woods. The views from open mountain slopes are spectacular.

1. From the parking lot, go to the kiosk that contains maps and general information about this region. From here, the trailhead is well marked and is just slightly uphill beyond the kiosk.

2. This is one of the best-marked networks of trails in the entire Okanagan Valley, so I will include only distances at major intersections. The first one comes within the first five minutes, and the signpost clearly indicates that you go straight.

3. Many marked and unmarked trails intersect with the main Lost Lake Trail. Routes with names like Fairlane Trail, Fairlane Loop, Upper Bench Trail, Galloping Trail and Salamander Trail criss-cross the main trail, but the way is always clearly marked.

4. Most of the elevation gain is acquired throughout the middle segment of this trek. The grade is almost unnoticeable, but there is no doubt that the net result is an increase of 256 m.

5. You will meet up with an important intersection at the 2.4-km mark, or 30–35 minutes from the trailhead. The "Teddy Bear" junction is distinguishable from all other forks or junctions on the trail (or anywhere else for that matter), as the trees around the junction are festooned with – you guessed it – teddy bears. This is quite an unusual, and somewhat creepy, sight to come across way back in the woods. Regardless of how it affects you, take the right-hand turn, continuing along the Pink Highway. From this point, most of the trail travels through the remnants of a forest that was destroyed during the 2003 fires.

6. The Pink Highway begins as a flat, single-track trail for almost 13 minutes (one kilometre) to where it reaches Natasha Trail, which veers to the right from the Pink Highway. Take this right turn and continue along Natasha Trail. Natasha is narrow and begins to descend slightly.

7. You will arrive at the intersection of Boris Trail, five to seven minutes along Natasha Trail. Continue straight along Natasha.

8. Almost a kilometre from the Natasha/Pink Highway intersection, the path brings you to the junction of Natasha and Bullwinkle trails. Take a right onto Bullwinkle. Much of the remaining

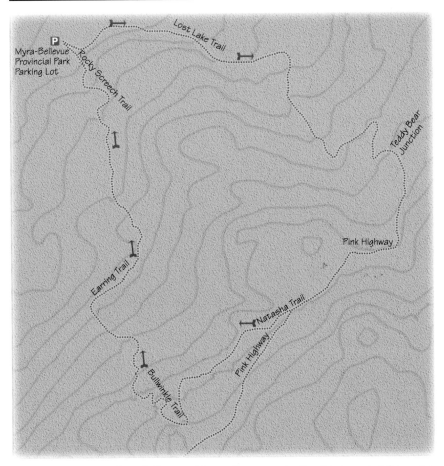

distance from here is downhill toward the parking lot.

9. The path intersects Boris Trail close to a kilometre (13–15 minutes) along Bullwinkle Trail. Take the left fork, maintaining course along Bullwinkle.

10. After a few minutes of easy hiking, you will arrive at a vital intersection where Bullwinkle Trail meets with Earring Trail. Take the right fork and continue your journey along Earring.

11. Five to seven minutes beyond this junction, you will come to a meeting of many trails. Earring, Big Drops and Connector trails all intersect at this point. Go straight and stay on Earring.

12. Earring Trail meets up with Upper Bench Trail ten minutes later. Take the right fork, and less than a minute later Rocky Screech Trail cuts through the path.

13. Go left down Rocky Screech Trail. You will soon come to a plateau where multiple trails meet. Stay right, heading downhill to the parking lot.

The open, grassy slopes of
the Pink Highway Loop allow
for extensive panoramas.

*Like many forests in the Kelowna area, this
one on the Pink Highway Loop has several
sturdy trees that, although scorched by the
fires of 2003, manage to stay upright.*

16. Lost Lake

Category: Return
Distance: 8.4 km round trip
Height gain: 256 m
High point: 792 m
Time: 2–3 hrs. round trip
Difficulty: Moderate
Seasons: Spring, summer, late fall
Trailhead coordinates: N49 48.738
    W119 26.558

Directions to trailhead: In Kelowna, at the intersection of Gordon Dr. and Highway 97, drive south on Gordon for 3.7 km to Casorso Rd. Turn left onto Casorso. Follow Casorso Rd. for 2.3 km as it goes through two traffic circles. At 2.3 km, the road splits into DeHart Rd. going right and Bedford Rd. going left – get onto Bedford Rd. Stay on Bedford for 1.4 km to where it intersects with Saucier Rd. and Stewart Rd. E. At this junction, Bedford Rd. terminates, so go straight onto Stewart Rd. E. In 1.5 km Stewart Rd. E. ends at the Myra-Bellevue Provincial Park parking lot.

This is a stroll that takes you through thin forests, burnt trees and open meadows. Lost Lake is more of a pond than a lake, but the tranquil setting makes it a popular destination.

1. From the parking lot, go to the kiosk, which contains maps and general information about this region. From here the trailhead is well marked and is just slightly uphill beyond the kiosk.

2. This is one of the best-marked networks of trails in the entire Okanagan Valley, so I will include only distances at major intersections. The first one comes within the first five minutes, and the signpost clearly says to go straight.

3. Many marked and unmarked trails intersect with the main Lost Lake trail. Routes with names like Fairlane Trail, Fairlane Loop, Upper Bench Trail, Galloping Trail and Salamander Trail criss-cross the main trail, but the way is always clearly marked.

4. Most of the elevation gain is acquired throughout the middle segment of this trek. The grade is almost unnoticeable, but there is no doubt that the net result is an increase of 256 m.

5. You will arrive at an important intersection at the 2.4-km mark, or 30–35 minutes from the trailhead. The "Teddy Bear" junction is distinguishable from all other forks or junctions on the trail (or anywhere else for that matter), as the trees around the junction are littered with – you guessed it – teddy bears. This is quite an unusual, and somewhat creepy, sight to come across way back in the woods. Regardless of how it affects you, take the left turn, continuing up the Lost Lake Trail.

6. More marked and unmarked trails intersect the Lost Lake Trail, but again the way is marked and obvious.

7. At 3.1 km, or roughly 50 minutes into the hike, you will come to a fork and its sign that needs your attention. One marker would send you continuing up Lost Lake Trail, while the other one directs you to the left to Lost Lake Loop (to Lost Lake). Go left onto a single-track trail.

8. Five minutes later you will arrive at another sign with two markers. One sends you along the Lost Lake Loop, while the other directs you to the left along the Spring By-Pass Route. Both of these trails meet up farther along the way. The Spring By-Pass Route does not refer to a spring of water but to a bypass that should be taken in springtime when water levels are high along the main trail.

9. After the two trails join together as

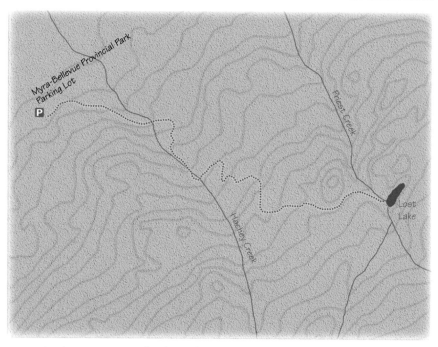

one again, it crosses a couple of wooden bridges in quick succession. The trail has reached its apex and the remainder of the hike is on flat ground.

10. Lost Lake is reached about five minutes from the bridges.

11. Return the same way.

Although this "Teddy Bear" junction is marked with adequate signage, it is also marked with a variety of teddy bears mounted on trees, logs, shrubs and signposts.

Stunning imagery awaits you on the trek to Lost Lake. This view is gazing to the west at West Kelowna on the shores of Okanagan Lake.

On the way to Lost Lake. Grasses and shrubs are the first vegetation to have gained a foothold in a forest that was devastated by fire in 2003.

Lost Lake is just a stone's throw from the main trail.

More of a pond than a lake, Lost Lake provides water for several species of wildlife in an environment where water is scarce.

17. Mission Creek Greenway – Ziprick Road to Field Road Section

Category: Through
Distance: 10.1 km
Height gain: 163 m
High point: 545 m
Time: 2.5–3 hrs. one way; 5–6 hrs. round trip
Difficulty: Strenuous
Seasons: Spring, summer, fall
Trailhead coordinates: N49 52.808 W119 25.080

Directions to trailhead: In Kelowna, at the intersection of Highway 97 and Leckie Rd., drive south on Leckie for 500 m to Springfield Rd. Turn left on Springfield and drive east for 700 m to Ziprick Rd. Turn right, into the Mission Creek Greenway parking lot.

This is a gorgeous hike alongside and high above a beautiful creek, its valley and its canyon. This is a section of the much longer Mission Creek Greenway Trail from Lakeshore Rd. to Field Rd. and consists of two phases that are now blended into a single 17.5-km walkway. I chose this section because it is much more scenic than the first 7.5 km of the walkway. Although that section is a convenient respite from the city, it is a flat, wide stretch of excessively used trail that really doesn't offer much challenge or nature. The last 10 km of the trail becomes progressively more difficult, wilder and less populated.

1. Get on the trail and immediately turn left; do not cross the bridge directly in front of you.

2. Within a minute, you will reach the only section of the trail where you travel on a residential road. This little trip through urban sprawl lasts six to seven minutes, after which the trail is picked up again at Gerstmar Park.

3. Back on the wide gravel path, you will see Mission Creek on your right and residential backyards on your left.

4. About 18–20 minutes later, you will come to a hydro station on your left. Just beyond that is the entrance to the trail at Hollywood Rd. S. Just up the trail from here, the route veers right and begins its journey away from suburban population.

5. About 30 minutes from the trailhead you will come to a fork in the path. The right fork travels beside a creek, while the left one enters an open meadow. Take the left fork.

6. At the far end of the meadow, cross East Kelowna Rd. On the other side of the road is a large parking lot. This is the official beginning of Phase 2 of the Mission Creek Greenway.

7. Once you leave the parking lot and rejoin the trail, the experience becomes more natural than suburban. Right away there is a small waterfall on the left and a swampy pond on the right. As the trail continues, it actually cuts right through a swamp.

8. The first of three bridges over Mission Creek is crossed within ten minutes from East Kelowna Rd. On the other side of the bridge you enter a wondrous dark forest of western red cedar and western hemlock.

9. The second bridge is crossed seven to eight minutes later.

10. Beyond this bridge, the path continues through the same beautiful woods for about ten minutes until it comes to a small rise to an opening. There is a portable

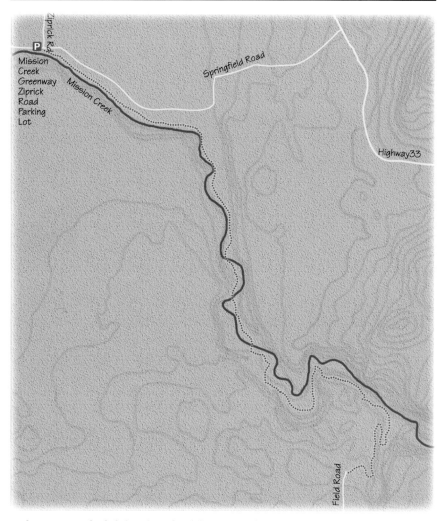

outhouse up to the left (north) side of this opening. There is a fork in the trail here as well – take the right fork.

11. A few minutes later you cross Mission Creek for the third and final time.

12. Just past the third bridge the route forks again. Stay on the main trail as it curves left and starts to climb. There is a sign here for the Grasslands Trail, sending you upward and to the left.

13. This ascent is made easier with the intermittent help of landscaping ties that have been converted into 72 stair steps. This type of stair construction is commonly used throughout the rest of the trail.

14. After a few minutes, the climb tops out on an open plateau with an abundance of panoramas.

15. The flatness of the plateau is enjoyed only briefly, as the descent down to the

This majestic rock outcropping is seen from a rest area at the 8-km mark of the Mission Creek Greenway –Ziprick Road to Field Road Section hike.

valley bottom begins shortly and is accomplished (with more landscaping ties) within five to seven minutes.

16. With all of this elevation gain and loss, the trail loses contact with the creek, and it takes another 15 minutes of wandering through the valley bottom before the trail meets up with the creek once again.

17. This union is broken after a few short minutes as the trail climbs back out of the valley. The climb to the next plateau takes six to eight minutes.

18. You will trek high above the creek for another six to eight minutes before you come to a large viewpoint with an information kiosk and benches. Sit down and enjoy the view of the canyon. You have earned it. You have completed 8 km of this hike.

19. The trail resumes at the other end of this open area and begins its journey

back down to the creek again. It takes six to eight minutes to reach the bottom of the canyon.

20. At the end of this descent is an intersection that is well marked. Going to the left will send you along Rock Ovens Trail, while going to the right will place you on Mission Creek Greenway Trail. Obviously, you want to take the right-hand trail.

21. For the next 20 minutes you gradually work your way out of the canyon to higher ground. You will come to an unmarked fork in the road. Take the right fork, which passes in front of a house. Immediately after passing the house, you will come to the Field Rd. parking lot.

22. Hopefully, you have made arrangements for a ride. Otherwise, enjoy the trek back to the Ziprick Rd. parking lot.

Most of the trail on the Ziprick Road to Field Road section of the Mission Creek Greenway trek exposes you to harsh sunlight on hot Okanagan summer days, so taking a break in a shaded forest becomes welcome.

One of many well maintained crossings over Mission Creek.

*The ever-gorgeous Mission Creek remains
at healthy water levels year round.*

*This serene pond is skirted shortly after
leaving the Phase 2 parking lot.*

18. Trepanier Creek Greenway

Category: Return
Distance: 6.4 km round trip
Height gain: 168 m
High point: 522 m
Time: 2–3 hrs. round trip
Difficulty: Moderate
Seasons: Spring, summer, late fall
Trailhead coordinates: N49 47.157
 W119 43.100

Directions to trailhead: From the west end of the William R. Bennett Bridge, travel approximately 20 km on Highway 97 to the town of Peachland. As you enter Peachland, watch for Clements Cres. on your right. There is a traffic light with a gas station on the right side of the highway at this intersection. Turn right onto Clements Cres. and follow it for 230 m. Parallel park on the street. The trailhead is on the left (west) side of a school.

This walk through a forest of Douglas fir and ponderosa pine provides fantastic views of Trepanier Creek and its canyon, as well as providing a little bit of history.

1. The trail begins as a flat, narrow path skirting the outside of a chain-link fence around an elementary school. Follow the trail to the far end of the school.

2. The path then turns uphill away from the school and begins to climb switchbacks.

3. As you ascend, look carefully down to your right, just off the trail, at the remains of an early settling reservoir built in 1909–1910 to remove floating particulate from the water before it reached the community below. This reservoir can be found at the 850-m mark of this hike.

Small cascades in Trepanier Creek are seen along the Trepanier Creek Greenway trail.

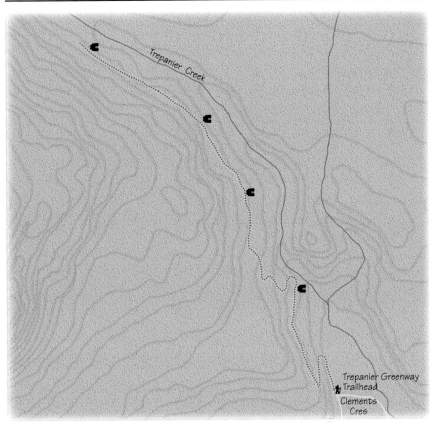

4. After ten minutes of climbing, the path levels off momentarily as it navigates through rubble caused by a landslide. This only lasts a couple of minutes.

5. Roughly 15 minutes into the hike, the trail splits. A fantastic viewpoint is found straight ahead, while the main trail makes a sharp left turn. Take the opportunity to deviate to the viewpoint; you won't be disappointed. Off in the distance are the remains of Peachland's first hydroelectric plant. Although it is non-functional, it now works as Trepanier Creek's man-made waterfall. At this junction the path begins to climb again.

6. Eight to ten minutes later, the footpath levels as it meets a T-junction. All the way,

so far, there have been small trail markers on trees. The image on these metal markers is a coniferous tree beside a winding stream. At this T-junction there is another one of these markers directing you to make a right turn. You have walked 1.4 km from the trailhead at this point.

7. From here on, the trail remains high above Trepanier Creek, which lies down to your right, with spectacular viewpoints along the way. Continue along this canyon edge stroll as far as you like, but at a little past the 3-km mark, the trail meets a Forest Service Road. Here is where you make a 180° turn and head back the same way you came.

Most of the Trepanier Creek Greenway hike
takes you through grasses and burnt forest.

Much of the Trepanier Creek Greenway hike
is slopeside with Trepanier Creek below.

19. Bear Creek Park – Canyon Rim Trail

Category: Loop
Distance: 3 km round trip
Height gain: 112 m
High point: 455 m
Time: 1–2 hrs. round trip
Difficulty: Easy
Seasons: Early spring, summer,
   late fall
Trailhead coordinates: N49 55.663
   W119 30.769

Directions to trailhead: On Harvey Ave. in downtown Kelowna, travel west to cross the William R. Bennett Bridge. At the west end of the bridge, take note of your odometer and travel 1.5 km on Highway 97 to the Westside Rd. exit. Drive 6.7 km north on Westside, following the signs to Bear Creek Provincial Park. The Canyon Rim Trail parking lot is on the left side.

This short, easy hike parallels the steep canyon rim of Lambly Creek, also known as Bear Creek. Vantage points presenting the steep, sudden drops of the canyon walls are the hike's highlight.

1. The single-track path starts as an uphill journey without switchbacks, with the canyon on your right and Okanagan Lake on your left.

2. Within the first ten minutes of climbing, the first glimpse of the canyon is presented, but only for a moment, as the trail soon veers to the left to continue its climb. Two sets of wooden stairs assist you in arriving at a spectacular view of Okanagan Lake while sitting on a comfortable bench.

3. The path now levels off as it goes through an open forest of pine. The canyon rim is now lined with a chain-link fence for your protection. The fence extends to strategic outcroppings, permitting fantastic viewpoints of the canyon below.

4. After 10 to 15 minutes of exploring the uppermost section of this loop hike, the path begins to descend toward Lambly Creek.

5. After crossing the river on a well-constructed bridge, the trek is at the apex of the loop and begins its journey back to the starting point.

6. The path undulates for a few minutes until you are greeted by a steep wooden staircase that takes two to three minutes to climb. There is a conveniently positioned outhouse at the top of the staircase on the left side.

7. You are now on level ground again for the next 15 minutes, with more fenced-in viewpoints along the way. You then begin to make your way down toward the parking lot.

8. The path descends via yet another wooden staircase to bring you to the bottom of the canyon. From here, select the left fork at a junction, taking you over a bridge back to your vehicle.

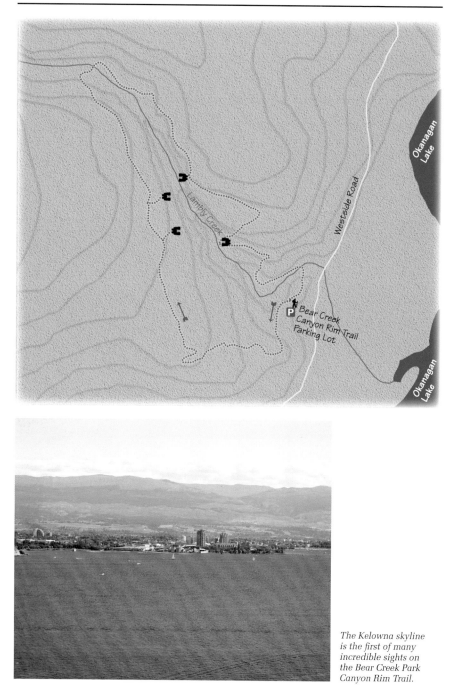

The Kelowna skyline is the first of many incredible sights on the Bear Creek Park Canyon Rim Trail.

The tumbling waters of Lambly Creek (also known as Bear Creek) add to the overall novelty of this unique canyon rim journey.

Lambly Creek canyon on a beautiful summer day. This is an absolutely specular hike considering its short distance of only 3 km.

*The jagged canyon walls of Lambly
Creek are the star attraction
on Canyon Rim Trail.*

*As Lambly Creek exits the canyon
it becomes much more docile.*

20. Blue Grouse Mountain

Category: Return
Distance: 13.6 km round trip
Height gain: 726 m
High point: 1277 m
Time: 2–3 hrs. round trip
Difficulty: Strenuous
Seasons: Spring, summer, fall
Trailhead coordinates: N49 56.197
　　W119 31.664

Directions to trailhead: On Harvey Ave., in downtown Kelowna, drive west to cross the William R. Bennett Bridge. At the west end of the bridge, take note of your odometer and travel 1.5 km to the Westside Rd. exit. Drive 8.1 km north on Westside and turn left onto Bear Lake Main road. This road is called "Lambly Rd." on Google Maps, Google Earth and Garmin's Basecamp mapping software, but you are looking for a street sign on top of a stop sign with the words "Bear Lk. Main." Oddly enough, if you zoom in on this intersection in Google Street View, the sign is clearly marked "Bear Lk Main." I guess even Google makes the occasional error. Regardless, drive 2 km up this road to a parking lot on the right side.

This trek provides great views of Okanagan Lake and downtown Kelowna, including the William R. Bennett Bridge. This exhausting hike gains 726 m of elevation within 6.8 km.

1. From the gravel parking lot, the trailhead is easily spotted at the south end. The trail begins as a rocky gravel road, and in fact the entire trail is a rough 4×4 road with very little clearance.

2. Within two minutes, you arrive in an open maze of multiple roads and trails. It is important that you take the road straight ahead up the discernible hillside. Observing the road going to the right at this intersection, you will see a small wooden structure in the distance that looks like an outhouse (it isn't). Do not take this road – take the next one to the left of it.

3. Three to four minutes later, you will come across many more roads – all heading upward. Some of these are shortcuts traversing the main road, but either way, they all meet farther up the main road. For simplicity's sake, this description and GPS data advise taking the main road without taking any shortcuts. Besides, most of the shortcuts are especially steep.

4. After 20 minutes of walking steadily uphill, the road appears as though it is avoiding the destination by heading northwest, while the summit seems to be far off behind you to the northeast. Yet soon enough it sets itself back on the correct course by making a sharp right, upward turn of about 80°.

5. The occasional shortcut continues to cross the main road. However, the way is obvious – stay on the main road and keep hiking uphill.

6. About 3 km into the trek, the road levels briefly, revealing spectacular views of Okanagan Lake off to your right.

7. As you continue to gain elevation again, you also gain greater frequency and duration of flat spots. This is welcome relief from all the elevation you've hiked so far.

8. At the 3.8-km mark, and roughly one hour into the hike, the road divides, but both forks merge about 20 m beyond the split.

9. Another junction with a signpost comes into play a few minutes later. The signpost informs you that this route is the "Easiest" – presumably, this is a

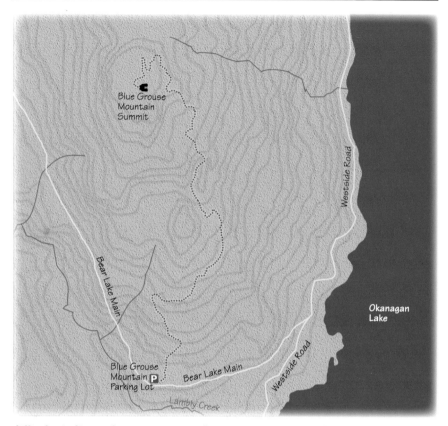

difficulty indicator for cross-country ski-ers. Additionally, this sign has markers pointing in almost all directions, with the numbers 1 and 14 listed. Despite what this signpost may want to tell you, take the left road.

10. The road resumes a steady climb. About 10–15 minutes later a road curves to the right, but you want to stay left on the main road, strolling under power lines a few minutes afterward.

11. Shortly beyond the power lines, you will encounter yet another fork in the road. The right branch takes you up to a communication tower, while the left one continues to climb for another 20–30 minutes to the summit of Blue Grouse Mountain.

12. From the communication tower road intersection, you have 1.5 km and 142 m of elevation to go. This remaining distance and height are uneventful, since there are no splits in the road, no scenery and no water – just the peaceful, rhythmic sound of your heart beating out of your chest.

13. The scenery from the summit of Blue Grouse Mountain is spectacular. Okanagan Lake and the city of Kelowna sprawl out in front of you as you gaze to the southeast.

*The summit of Blue Grouse Mountain presents
spectacular vistas. The great expanse of Okanagan
Lake is evident as you look southward.*

*Again from the top of Blue Grouse Mountain.
This photo shows the William R. Bennett
Bridge and part of downtown Kelowna.*

*Still more spectacular sights from Blue Grouse
Mountain. The top photo is a view looking to the east,
while the bottom photo presents an endless sky and
a seemingly endless Okanagan Lake looking north.*

21. Carrot Mountain Bluffs

Category: Return
Distance: 5.2 km round trip
Height gain: 574 m
High point: 1204 m
Time: 2.5–3.5 hrs. round trip
Difficulty: Moderately strenuous
Seasons: Late spring, summer, fall
Trailhead coordinates: N49 52.304
   W119 36.803

This is a straightforward, upward climb taking you to 1204 m above sea level, overlooking West Kelowna, Shannon Lake and the much larger Okanagan Lake. Exactly 574 m are gained on a 21.6 per cent grade in 2.6 km, so come prepared for a good workout.

Directions to trailhead: On Harvey Ave. in downtown Kelowna, drive west to cross the William R. Bennett Bridge. At the west end of the bridge, take note of your odometer and travel 6 km to Bartley Rd. Turn right onto Bartley. About 300 m down Bartley, turn left onto Shannon Lake Rd. and continue for 1.6 km until you reach Shannon Woods Dr. Go right onto Shannon Woods. Now look for Shannon Hills Dr., approximately 800 m up the road. Take a right turn to get onto Shannon Hills Dr. The final "Shannon" on this route is discovered shortly: turn left onto Shannon Heights Pl. and park at the end of the cul-de-sac. The gravel road trail is on the right.

1. Right away, the gravel road approaches a large, cylindrical water reservoir. The reservoir's concrete top is at path height and must be crossed to find the trail at the far end. Now a single-track trail, the route heads into thick forest and begins a moderate ascent. The path parallels a gully on its right.

2. The grade becomes steeper about 15 minutes into the hike, and the route crosses the gully twice before the grade eventually lessens 10–15 minutes later.

3. Some 1.5 km, or about 30 minutes, from the trailhead, the path crosses in front of a small waterfall. In late summer this fall gradually diminishes to just some water running down a mossy rock wall.

4. Still clambering up this persistent uphill trek, you find the trail breaks through the forest to a broad, grassy slope dotted with western hemlock roughly 2 km, or 45–60 minutes, from the trailhead.

5. The grade diminishes now for the remaining 20 minutes, as the trail winds modestly to the summit. This remaining push to the peak has welcome flat spots, some beautiful views and a mixture of forest and grasslands, but the breathtaking views at the top are what make this trek truly rewarding.

6. The summit of Carrot Mountain Bluffs is unmistakably marked with a raised Canadian flag.

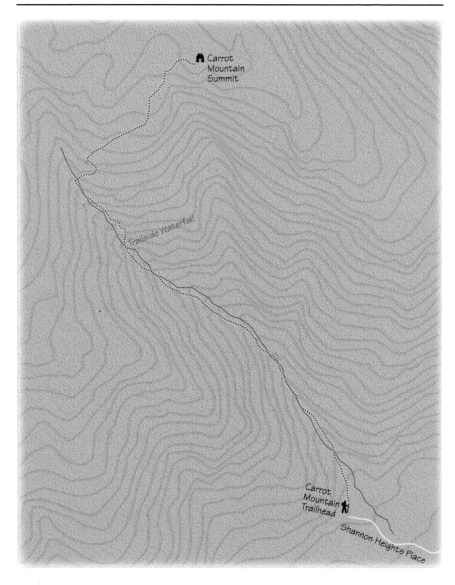

Carrot Mountain Summit

Trailside Waterfall

Carrot Mountain Trailhead

Shannon Heights Place

The route to the summit of Carrot Mountain Bluffs starts in a thick, dank forest but eventually culminates on a bare mountaintop.

The Canadian flag on the summit of Carrot Mountain Bluffs was an unexpected bonus.

22. Mount Boucherie

Category: Return
Distance: 3.8 km round trip
Height gain: 291 m
High point: 756 m
Time: 2–3 hrs. round trip
Difficulty: Moderately strenuous
Seasons: Spring, summer, fall
Trailhead coordinates: N49 51.531
W119 34.801

In the busy heart of West Kelowna stands a stellar mountain that can be seen from many kilometres away, yet most people in the area have never made their way to the summit. Vistas of Kelowna, West Kelowna and Okanagan Lake make this short, but tough, climb worthy of your efforts.

Directions to trailhead: On Highway 97 in downtown Kelowna, drive west to cross the William R. Bennett Bridge. At the west end of the bridge, take note of your odometer and travel 5.3 km to Ross Rd. Turn left onto Ross Rd. Follow Ross for 500 m and turn left on Hewl Rd. Drive about 200 m to arrive at the Mount Boucherie Complex parking lot, in particular, the Jim Lind Arena parking lot. Turn left into the gravel lot and drive to the farthest part of the east end of it. The trailhead is readily found as it departs the parking lot and heads into a forest.

1. The trail is a single-track path that cuts through a forest of spruce, larch and hemlock. At the trailhead, take the left fork and commence ascending immediately.

2. About five minutes into the climb, a few shortcut trails depart from the main route, but please remain on the main trail to avoid eroding the hillside.

3. The trail continues to climb through a changing landscape of forest and low brush for about a kilometre, where it intersects at a significant junction. At this intersection, a distinctively skinny larch tree has faint markings of directional arrows on it. Make sure you take the right-hand fork, which continues to climb the hillside. You have climbed 140 m of 291, leaving you with 151 m of elevation remaining.

4. After taking the right-hand fork, you will immediately come to a slope of loose talus. Crossing over the talus only takes a couple of minutes.

5. Vistas of Okanagan Lake, Highway 97 and the city of Kelowna begin to come into view.

6. Five or six minutes from the first talus slope, you need to cross another narrow band of loose rubble, again taking a couple of minutes to do so.

7. The trail passes some rocky outcroppings and traverses one last belt of scree before yielding to a grassy slope with a milder incline. Now the summit is only a few minutes ahead of you.

8. A demanding climb should compensate a day hiker with spectacular scenery, and this climb certainly delivers on this decree. There are fabulous sights all around you, but the best views are to the east.

Although West Kelowna has developed rapidly (including mountainsides) over the past decade, it is refreshing to see an abundance of unclaimed forests and hilltops that have, so far, avoided the developer's hammer. Such is the view from the summit of Mount Boucherie.

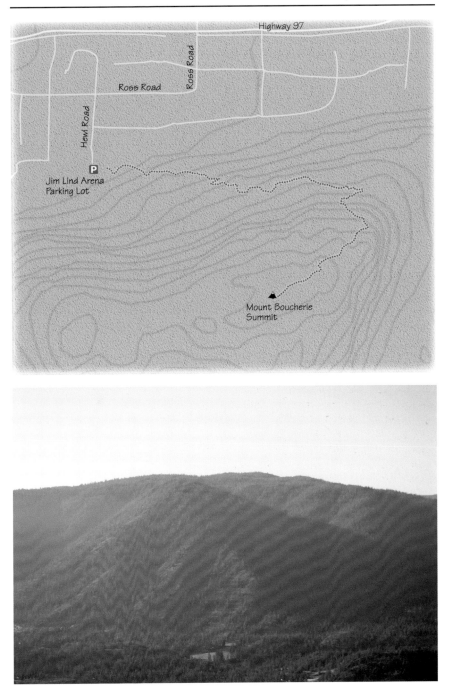

The hike to the summit of Mount Boucherie has a variety of vegetation, including pesky dense bush like this.

The top of Mount Boucherie reveals fantastic scenery in all directions, but the views to the east are the most spectacular.

Looking northeast from the summit of Mount Boucherie.

Another broad vista to the east from the top of Mount Boucherie.

23. McDougall Rim Viewpoints

Category: Return
Distance: 10.6 km round trip
Height gain: 463 m
High point: 1091 m
Time: 3–4 hrs. round trip
Difficulty: Strenuous
Seasons: Late spring, summer, fall
Trailhead coordinates: N49 53.082
    W119 35.244

Directions to trailhead: On Harvey Ave. in downtown Kelowna, drive west to cross the William R. Bennett Bridge. At the west end of the bridge, take note of your odometer and travel 6 km to Bartley Rd. Turn right onto Bartley Rd. About 300 m down Bartley, turn left onto Shannon Lake Rd. Bartley Rd. intersects Shannon Lake Rd. again after about 200 m. Turn right, back onto Bartley. Drive along Bartley for 2.2 km to a dirt parking lot on the right side of what has now become a gravel road.

There is a lot of elevation gain at the start of this trek, but you are rewarded with three astonishing viewpoints along an exhilarating ridge walk.

1. The trail immediately begins as an uphill grind and will continue this way for most of the journey. There are multiple trails that switchback, but there is a 4×4 road that goes straight up. The choice is yours. This guy always picks the easiest route, even if it takes longer, so for the description of this trek, I chose the switchback option.

2. Regardless of your choice, all trails culminate in a single solitary uphill path about 1 km, or 15 minutes, into the trip. The environment thus far has consisted of hilly grassland dotted with pine trees, but

where the trails converge, the path enters denser forest.

3. Just past an old 2-km marker the grade lessens but the trail is still going skyward. The reduced pitch lasts for about a kilometre, then finally levels off at the first spectacular viewpoint.

4. From here the trail rolls up and down, with some flat spots, but the overall sum of this rolling is more height gain.

5. You will come to the second viewpoint about 1.3 km (20–25 minutes) from the first. All the while, you have been skirting the edge of a high cliff on your right that provides ongoing vantage points for scenery. Just prior to arriving at this viewpoint, you will come to a T-intersection at a 4×4 road. Turn right onto the road.

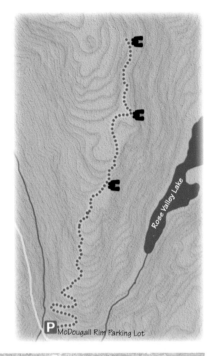

Rose Valley Lake in the foreground and Okanagan Lake in the background from the McDougall Rim Viewpoints hike.

6. The second viewpoint is equipped with a picnic table, enabling you to rest your weary legs while taking in the sights of Okanagan Lake to the east and Rose Valley Lake directly beneath you.

7. The road continues to hug the ridgeline for about another kilometre to another sensational vantage point. Here the trail leaves the ridgeline and heads into a forest. Feel free to continue from here, but I have ventured roughly three kilometres beyond this point and it is simply a walk in the woods. There is nothing wrong with a walk in the woods, but there doesn't appear to be much of anything beyond this. Other sources claim that the true McDougall Rim walk is a 20-km round trip, and it probably is, but I don't know what it has to offer.

Downtown Kelowna and the William R. Bennett Bridge from one of the viewpoints on the McDougall Rim Viewpoints trail.

24. *Kalamoir Regional Park*

Category: Loop
Distance: 3.6 km round trip
Height gain: 78 m
High point: 425 m
Time: 1–2 hrs. round trip
Difficulty: Moderate
Seasons: Early spring, summer,
    late fall
Trailhead coordinates: N49 50.750
    W119 32.821

This short hike provides splendid views of Okanagan Lake and slope-side walks through grasslands, but the chief geological allure is the remnants of volcanic activity strewn throughout the park.

Directions to trailhead: On Highway 97 in downtown Kelowna, drive west to cross the William R. Bennett Bridge. At the west end of the bridge, take note of your odometer and travel 2.6 km, turning left onto Boucherie Rd. Drive 1.4 km to Stuart Rd. Turn left onto Stuart and drive 750 m to Thacker Dr. Turn right onto Thacker. After 1.1 km, turn right at Collens Hill Rd. Very quickly, Collens Hill Rd. takes an abrupt right curve. Follow Collens Hill Rd. downward for 1 km to the lakeside parking lot.

1. The park trail system consists of three interlocking trails. The lowest in elevation is the Waterfront Trail, while the two upper trails are the Upper Rim and Mike Passmore trails. Start this trek with an immediate climb up a single-track trail, which levels off within five minutes of hiking. This is the Waterfront Trail.

2. The trek soon becomes a walk on a grassy hillside with the high ground on your right side. You will pass by some of this park's gifts of volcanic debris on the uphill side right away.

3. An advantage of a clear hillside trek is the vistas that are granted without obstruction, and this is fully presented within 2–3 minutes from the trailhead. Straight ahead as you look south, Okanagan Lake overshadows everything around you.

4. A minor junction is encountered 7–8 minutes from the trailhead, with a fork going up to the right, but the main trail, which you should stay on, continues straight.

5. A few minutes later, a park sign and information stand are visible. Take a right at a fork in the trail just as these come into view. You have now left the Waterfront Trail and have joined the Upper Rim Trail. The path here is narrower and ascends moderately.

6. A few minutes later you will come to another fork in the trail. The path going downhill on the right is the same one that left the trail on the right earlier. Stay on the upper path, staying straight.

7. Roughly 1 km into the hike the first of two park benches, which are five minutes apart, appears on your left.

8. Past the second bench, the trail descends slightly for about five minutes until it crosses the road you drove down to the parking lot (Collens Hill Rd.).

9. The trail continues to go downward on the other side of the road for a couple of minutes until it comes to a faint fork in the trail. Although the fork going up to the left is unmarked, and indistinguishable from any other trail, it is in fact the south end of the Mike Passmore Trail. If you miss this and carry on down the main trail, you will simply arrive back at the Waterfront Trail sooner rather than later.

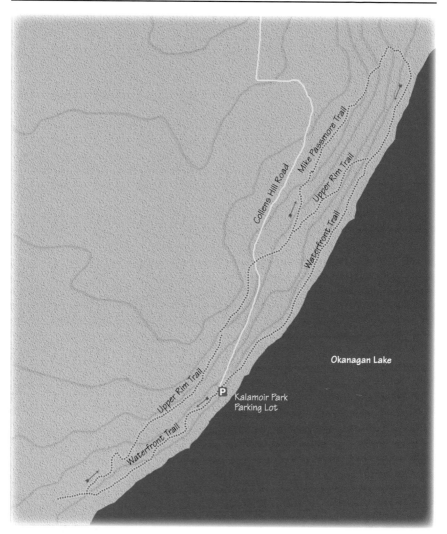

10. After five minutes of hiking on the Mike Passmore Trail, you begin to descend toward the lake, making your way from the upper grassland slopes through a sparse forest of western hemlock.

11. About 45 minutes from the trailhead, Mike Passmore Trail intersects with Waterfront Trail. Make a right turn here, and hike about 1 km back to the parking lot on a level, delightful, lakeside stroll along the Waterfront Trail.

The scenic Kalamoir Regional Park trek grants a variety of landscapes, from dry, grassy slopes to lush forests such as this one.

Volcanic rock is one of the main attractions on the Kalamoir Regional Park trails.

95

*Eroded volcanic rock along the trail
in Kalamoir Regional Park.*

*Splendid scenery is abundant while strolling
lakeside in Kalamoir Regional Park.*

25. Pincushion Mountain

Category: Return
Distance: 4.2 km round trip
Height gain: 246 m
High point: 812 m
Time: 1–2 hrs. round trip
Difficulty: Moderate
Seasons: Spring, summer, late fall
Trailhead coordinates: N49 47.318
    W119 44.053

Early in the 20th century, a fire ravaged the slopes of this mountain, leaving burnt, black trees in its wake, giving the appearance of pins in a cushion, hence the name "Pincushion Mountain." This is a quick hike, with significant elevation gain. Scenery from the summit, and the summit ridge, makes this a popular hike.

Directions to trailhead: From the west end of the William R. Bennett Bridge, travel approximately 20 km on Highway 97 to the town of Peachland. As you enter Peachland, watch for Ponderosa Dr. on your right. You really can't miss it, though, since there is a giant golf ball resting on a giant tee just before it. The sign is a marker for Ponderosa Golf & Country Club, near the top of Ponderosa Dr. Drive 2.8 km up windy Ponderosa Dr. to a signed gravel parking lot on the right.

1.   This hike begins as a single-track path with a climb up two staircases totalling about 50–60 timber steps. Very quickly, views of Okanagan Lake and Peachland come into play.

2.   Just beyond the top of the stairs, a sign sends you to the right, where the trail changes to an old Forest Service Road. The route is now level, but only for a couple of minutes.

3.   While enjoying your stroll on the flat road, watch for a single-track trail on the left, going into the woods. This exit from the road is marked with a sign with a left-pointing arrow, the number "3" and the single word, "Pincushion." Get on this trail.

4.   The trail now begins to test your cardiovascular fitness by presenting you with a series of switchbacks with intermittent flat spots. This entire hike gains 246 m in a 2.1-km distance, giving it a grade of 11.7 per cent.

5.   About 15 minutes from the trailhead, there is a fantastic viewpoint off the right side of the trail. Take a break and enjoy the scenery – after all, scenery is what you came here for.

6.   About 30–40 minutes into the hike, the path navigates quickly through a few large boulders, but the route is quite evident, the path well trodden.

7.   After picking your way through this, you will find yourself on a ridge heading uphill toward the summit.

8.   With the forest thinning out, spectacular vistas of Peachland, Okanagan Lake, and Okanagan Mountain across the lake come into view.

9.   Continue on the ridge for another few minutes to the summit of Pincushion Mountain. In the summer of 2013 there was a beautiful Canada flag flapping in the breeze, marking the top of the mountain.

10. The south panorama of Okanagan Lake appears endless as it winds its way to its southern end at Penticton. Directly below you, the picturesque town of Peachland spreads out from the shoreline toward the hillsides. Behind you to the west, rocky crags and gorges make sure you go back the same way that brought you here.

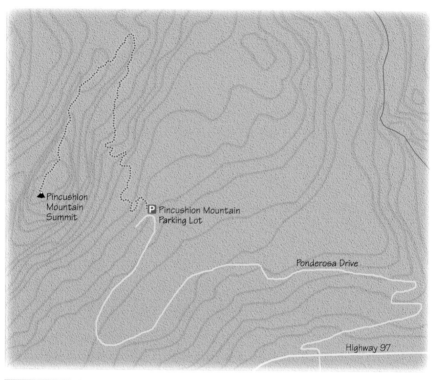

▲ Pincushion
Mountain
Summit

🅿 Pincushion Mountain
Parking Lot

Ponderosa Drive

Highway 97

*Okanagan Lake seen
from the summit of
Pincushion Mountain.*

Okanagan Lake and Squally Point looking south from the top of Pincushion Mountain.

Treed hillsides and mountaintops occupy the west panoramas of Pincushion Mountain.

26. Rose Valley Regional Park – Upper Loop

Category: Loop
Distance: 4.6 km round trip
Height gain: 222 m
High point: 796 m
Time: 1.5–2.5 hrs. round trip
Difficulty: Moderate
Seasons: Spring, summer, fall
Trailhead coordinates: N49 53.063
   W119 33.616

Directions to trailhead: On Harvey Ave. in downtown Kelowna, travel west and cross the William R. Bennett Bridge. At the west end of the bridge, take note of your odometer and travel 2.7 km to Horizon Dr. Turn right onto Horizon and travel 3.3 km to Westlake Rd. The parking lot for Rose Valley Regional Park is about 300 m down Westlake Rd., on the right (north) side of the road.

This fantastic loop hike gets the heart pounding right away but puts the hard climbing behind you within the first 30 minutes. The remainder of the hike is a breeze.

1. From the parking lot, go through the gap in the fence and take the road heading straight ahead and upward. Do not take the road going to the right.

2. The journey begins with a rather serious climb for five to ten minutes, but the grade eventually lessens briefly and you will find yourself in a sparse forest of western larch and lodgepole pine. After this short-lived respite, the road begins to climb again.

3. As you continue on this upward trek, there will be notable roads and bike paths crossing your way. However, continue straight up the gravel road you started your journey on.

4. Roughly 20 minutes into the hike, you emerge from the forest, where you are presented with spectacular views of Kelowna and Okanagan Lake to your right. The road now becomes a rocky path and soon you will begin walking on a broad ridge.

5. Within 30 minutes, you have reached the top of the ridge at the 1.5-km mark, which is the summit of this trek. A couple of minutes after realizing the summit, you will be greeted with an appropriately placed bench for resting and viewing after such a strenuous half-hour hike. You have gained 222 m in elevation. The remainder of this hike is either level or downhill.

6. Continue past the bench. The trail rolls as it wraps around behind boulders, and there are even a couple of staircases carved into the rock. This is quite unexpected, but someone has certainly put in significant time and effort to make this trek slightly easier.

7. There is another viewing bench just four or five minutes past the first one. This one is positioned to enhance the views to the north and northwest.

8. After you have rested on this bench and enjoyed the splendid scenery, carry on down the trail as it drops slightly to signs providing routes and destinations for this multi-trail system. Turn right at the signs, placing you on a single-track trail. Much of the remainder of this trek is on mountain bike trails, so be cognizant of bikers flying down the hill behind you.

9. Within five or six minutes of taking this trail downward, it levels off into a vast meadow.

10. Another 4–5 minutes brings you to a T-junction intersecting a wide trail. Take the right fork.

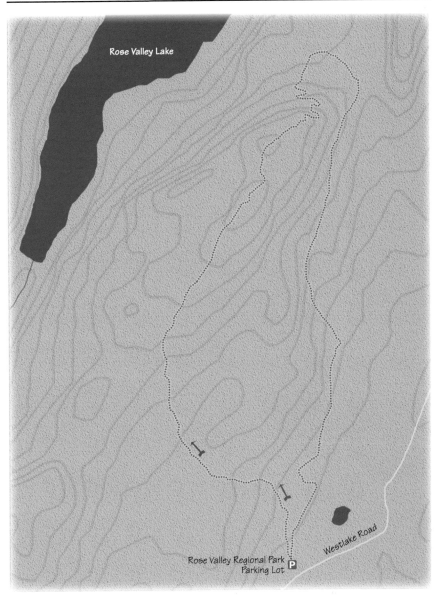

11. Immediately, you will come to more signs. These designate the park boundary, as well as informing you that if you continue on the main trail you will be entering private property. Consequently, take the single-track trail to your right. It is well marked with ribbons, homemade signs and arrows made of wood – you cannot miss it. You are now back in an open forest.

12. Carry on along this single-track bike trail, which reveals residential houses on your left.

13. Roughly ten minutes beyond the park boundary sign, you will come to an unmarked fork in the trail. There is a faint trail that continues straight. You need to take the more used trail travelling downward to the left. You have now been walking for about an hour, or 3.5 km, from the trailhead.

14. You will encounter a similar intersection within another five minutes. The same advice applies: you should take the trail on the left, which is more trampled. You should see a small marker on a tree indicating you are on Yellow Bell Loop Trail.

15. A couple of minutes later, you will come to a small clearing with a picnic table and trail going to a paved road. This is one of several entrances into the park. Resume your course, passing the picnic table into the forest, always checking for the markers on trees keeping you on Yellow Bell Loop Trail.

16. The final significant intersection occurs approximately ten minutes beyond the picnic table. A trail crosses perpendicular to you. Take the trail that is 90° to your left, once again looking for small Yellow Bell Loop Trail markers on the trees. There is an abundance of these markers.

17. Almost immediately after taking this left turn, you will come to a gravel path. Turning right on this gravel path will take you past a school and a pond on your left, delivering you back to the parking lot within five minutes.

It seems like you can see forever, looking north from the Rose Valley Regional Park – Upper Loop trail.

Open grasslands are plentiful as you make your way on the Rose Valley Regional Park – Upper Loop journey.

Residential areas are constantly encroaching on wilderness in West Kelowna as you can see in this photo from the uppermost point of the Rose Valley Regional Park – Upper Loop hike.

*The serene Rose Valley Lake lies
within Rose Valley Regional Park.*

*The Rose Valley Regional Park – Upper Loop
hike offers a feast of vistas in all directions.
This view is seen looking to the northeast.*

27. Rose Valley Regional Park – Rose Valley Lake

Category: Return
Distance: 6 km round trip
Height gain: 129 m
High point: 688 m
Time: 1.5–2.5 km round trip
Difficulty: Easy
Seasons: Early spring, summer,
    late fall
Trailhead coordinates: N50 27.711
    W119 16.102

Directions to trailhead: On Harvey Ave. in downtown Kelowna, travel west and cross the William R. Bennett Bridge. At the west end of the bridge, take note of your odometer and travel 2.7 km to Horizon Dr. Turn right onto Horizon and travel for 3.3 km to Westlake Rd. The parking lot for Rose Valley Regional Park is about 300 m down Westlake Rd., on the right (north) side of the road.

This is an easy hike that takes you to a gorgeous lake in an equally gorgeous surrounding.

1. To start this trek, go through the opening in a wire fence to an information kiosk. Take the first trail on your right and head north.

2. The journey starts in a hillside forest of ponderosa pine and Douglas fir, with the uphill side on your left. Within the first minute you will meet a fork in the trail. Take the right-hand branch, maintaining a course that is low toward the fenceline.

3. Within another minute there will be a wonderful little pond on your right. A couple of minutes beyond the pond, you will go by a school, also on your right. Here you will meet another junction, and once again you will take the right-hand branch, staying low.

4. Seven or eight minutes into the trek the trail veers to the left, away from the school, and starts its uphill journey.

5. Four or five minutes later you will see houses on your right, and another fork in the trail. The left, more travelled branch is the one you should choose. Keep in mind that this hike begins on Yellow Bell Loop Trail, so watch for small signs containing a yellow bell flower.

6. The path will soon connect with another trail. At this junction there is a map of the area and a picnic table. Stay on this obvious main trail.

7. The path climbs through the forest for about 15 minutes, and at the 1.8-km mark it flattens and reaches a T-junction with some signs. The most notable one is the park boundary sign. Take a left turn here and follow the trail as it becomes more exposed through open rangeland.

8. Within a couple of minutes, the lake comes into view and the trail begins its drop down to Rose Valley Lake.

9. You will arrive at the lake 10–15 minutes later.

10. There are a couple of vantage points that allow fantastic north and south vistas of this rather large, glacier-formed lake. Although the natural makeup of the lake is a result of glacial carving, it has been augmented to create a man-made reservoir.

11. Return the same way.

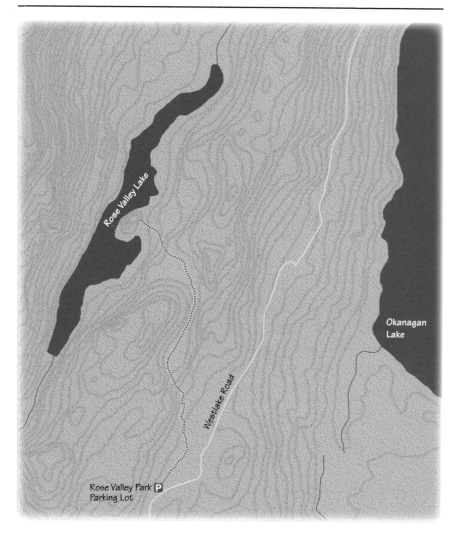

*Looking north up Rose Valley Lake
from the east shoreline.*

*The approach to Rose Valley Lake is
down a gentle grass slope. You see
the lake long before you arrive at it.*

The waters of Rose Valley Lake were particularly calm during a recent visit, offering mirror images of the surrounding beauty.

Rose Valley Lake is home to many species of waterfowl, including this lone female mallard.

28. Giant's Head Mountain Park

Category: Return
Distance: 6 km round trip
Height gain: 288 m
High point: 840 m
Time: 1.5–2.5 hrs. round trip
Difficulty: Moderately strenuous
Seasons: Spring, summer, fall
Trailhead coordinates: N49 35.840
    W119 40.557

Directions to trailhead: Seventeen kilometres north of Penticton, in the town of Summerland, look for the traffic-controlled intersection of Highway 97 and Rosedale Ave. Drive south (left) on Rosedale for 800 m to get to Prairie Valley Rd. Turn left on Prairie Valley and drive for 200 m to Giants Head Rd. Turn right onto Giants Head and drive 550 m to reach Milne Rd. Turn right onto Milne and go another 550 m to reach the roadside pullover parking spots on the left.

This is a popular hike with the local populous, and it always seems to be busy. There is a good reason for this trail to be busy, though, as there are sensational 360° views at the summit.

1. This is a rather straightforward hike, as the trail is a narrow road that goes most of the way to the top of the mountain. Most of the traffic on this route is either hikers or cyclists. There is the occasional vehicle that drives the narrow road to the upper parking lot, but generally speaking this is a pedestrian/cycling road.

2. The road begins by making its way through the park gates and immediately opens up to a grassy slope mixed with wildflowers, depending on the time of year. Views of Okanagan Lake are evident right away.

3. This walk is a climb with only a few breaks in the uphill drudgery, and the first one comes about 1 km into the hike. This flat spot lasts for a couple of minutes and is a welcome reprieve. You have gained 88 m of elevation to this point. There is a park bench at the far end of this spot, providing some stellar panoramas of Okanagan Lake.

There are many park benches and picnic tables throughout the entire park.

4. Switchback left and continue to climb.

5. At the 2-km mark, another park bench awaits your weary bones, once again supplying you with fantastic vistas.

6. The end of the pavement is reached within 35–40 minutes of hiking, at the upper parking lot. There are a couple of places to stop and rest in this parking lot.

7. The main trail leaves the right (west) side of the parking lot and is identified by a few boulders intent on impeding further vehicular traffic. The route is a single-track, firm trail, which is unique compared to the many shortcuts that litter the upper reaches of Giant's Head Mountain. Please avoid the temptation to use these shortcut routes, as trampling off of the main designated trail causes long-term damage to the native foliage. Besides, the main trail has wide-sweeping switchbacks that inevitably make the remaining 58 m of ascent significantly easier.

8. You will arrive at the summit 10–15 minutes after leaving the upper parking lot.

9. The extent of the Okanagan Valley's agriculture is revealed from this viewpoint, with vineyards and fruit orchards spread out below you. Okanagan Lake steals the show looking east.

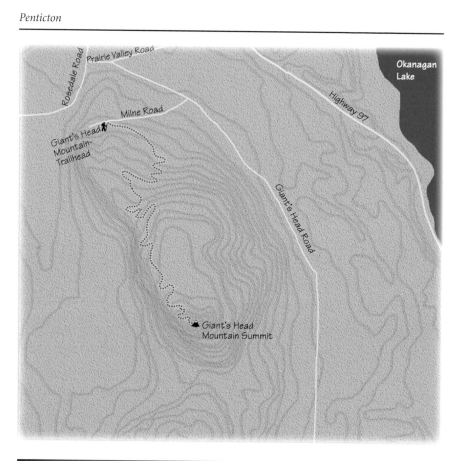

Rosedale Road
Prairie Valley Road
Okanagan Lake
Highway 97
Milne Road
Giant's Head Mountain Trailhead
Giant's Head Road
Giant's Head Mountain Summit

From the top of Giant's Head Mountain Park one can see a busy Okanagan Lake on a hot summer day, with the town of Naramata on the eastern shore.

*Scenery is abundant on the paved
walk up to the summit of Giant's Head.
Okanagan Lake stretches to the north.*

*The town of Summerland viewed on the way
to the top of Giant's Head Mountain Park.*

111

The distinct wake of watercraft shows there were a lot of people playing on Okanagan Lake this beautiful day.

The green rectangular patches seen from Giant's Head summit demonstrate the diversity of agriculture in this region. Fruit orchards often grow alongside vineyards and vegetable fields.

29. Skaha Bluffs Scenic Route

Category: Return with an end loop
Distance: 4.5 km round trip
Height gain: 112 m
High point: 613 m
Time: 1.5 hrs. round trip
Difficulty: Easy
Seasons: Spring, summer, late fall
Trailhead coordinates: N49 25.873
    W119 33.874

Directions to trailhead: In the city of Penticton, at the intersection of Industrial Ave. W. and S. Main St., follow S. Main for 3.3 km to where it becomes Lakeside Rd. Continue on Lakeside for 2.7 km to Smythe Dr. Turn left onto Smythe and drive along this narrow paved road to the Skaha Bluffs Provincial Park parking lot.

Mainly a rock climber's paradise, Skaha Bluffs offers multiple hiking trails among its glut of rock walls. This chosen route takes you on a walk through open grassland to the foot of vertical limestone walls and to viewpoints of Skaha Lake.

1. From the uppermost parking lot, walk back down the road a very short distance until you come to the first information kiosk. There will be a sign directing you into the bushes to "Daycare."

2. The trail begins as an old service road but comes to an end, becoming a single-track path at an intersection within the first five minutes of the hike. Take the right fork at this first minor intersection. Ahead of you, some rock walls begin to come into view.

3. A few minutes on the single-track path brings you to another fork. This is unmarked and not quite as obvious as the previous one. Stay straight (left) to stay on the main trail.

4. Shortly afterward, again stay straight along your course where a sign to the right tries to send you to "Diamondback."

5. Fifteen minutes into the hike brings you to a well-marked intersection. Go left, following the signed marker to "Wave." Take note that this is where the end loop of

this trek begins and to which it ultimately returns.

6. Immediately after turning left, you will go up and over some exposed rocks. Look down to your right to see a sign sending you to Wave and "Fortress." Follow this path as it takes you down to the bottom of a shallow gully.

7. As you come out of the gully on the other side, turn right at a fork and climb up a rock slab staircase, following a sign to the Red Trail.

8. At the top of the rock staircase you will reach the base of the Fortress rock-climbing area. Continue straight as you skirt the base of this enormous rock wall.

9. About 30 minutes, or 2 km, into the hike, you will come to a solar-powered outhouse. Go past the outhouse, maintaining a straight trajectory up and over some exposed boulders.

10. You will arrive at a noteworthy intersection a couple of minutes later. At this junction, take the right fork where the signs direct you toward "Go Anywhere" and "Great Whale." Prior to taking this path, you can take a side journey and head to your left to a rocky outcropping that provides splendid viewing of Skaha Lake.

11. Now, back to the trail. By taking the right fork, you will descend briefly into the bottom of a gully, only to come out the other side, climbing upward for about 6–8 minutes.

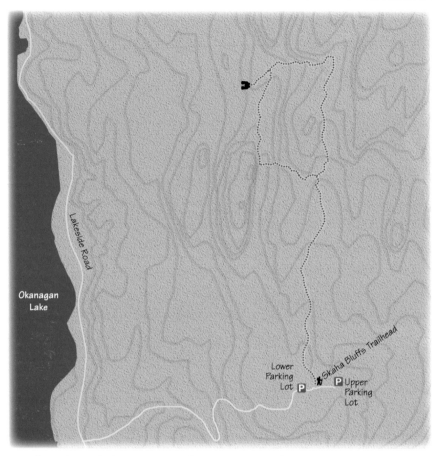

12. Where the trail plateaus, turn right at a fork where a sign sends you to "Blazing Buttress." This stroll through open grassland, which is dotted with the occasional pine tree, gives up scenery of magnificent rock walls on your left and Skaha Lake on your right.

13. Ten minutes from the Blazing Buttress sign brings you to a T-junction, where you will follow the "Great White" sign directions guiding you to your right.

14. A couple of minutes later, you are back at the loop intersection, with a little over a kilometre of hiking to return you to the parking lot.

Take a break onto a rocky outcrop and enjoy vistas of Skaha Lake while exploring the Skaha Bluffs Scenic Route. Power lines remind that you are never far from civilization while hiking in the South Okanagan.

Downtown Penticton can be seen from many vantage points in Skaha Bluffs Provincial Park.

For the most part, the hike through Skaha Bluffs Provincial Park is open forest, grasslands and rock – lots of rock.

One of many rock bluffs enjoyed by throngs of climbers in Skaha Bluffs Provincial Park.

30. Rock Ovens Park

Category: Return
Distance: 20 km round trip
Height gain: 324.4 m
High point: 913.8 m
Time: 5–6 hrs. round trip
Difficulty: Easy
Seasons: Spring, summer, late fall
Trailhead coordinates: N49 35.777
    W119 34.120

Directions to trailhead: In downtown Penticton, from the intersection of Main St. and Eckhardt Ave. W., drive 800 m east on Eckhardt and turn left on Haven Hill Rd. Travel Haven Hill for about 300 m and turn right onto Johnson Rd. One kilometre along Johnson brings you to a sweeping 90° left turn. Johnson Rd. continues straight, becoming a minor route, while the main road now becomes Upper Bench Rd. Continue on Upper Bench for 1.7 km to a stop sign at McMillan Rd. Turn right onto McMillan, following the signs to Naramata.

Very quickly McMillan Rd. makes a 90° left turn and changes into Naramata Rd. Travel this scenic route for 9.7 km. At 9.7 km, Naramata Rd. continues to the right as N. Naramata Rd., a lesser route. The main road continues on a wide leftward curve as Robinson Ave. Take N. Naramata Rd., and roughly 500 m later, go right on Smethurst Rd.

Continue up Smethurst for 1.2 km as it narrows and winds its way up through lovely vineyards. The gravel parking lot is obvious, just beyond the railway-crossing sign.

The rock ovens were constructed between 1911 and 1915 during the height of railway construction in this area. They were created to make life in the labour camps tolerable, allowing cooks to bake fresh bread for the work crews every day. There are 13 rock ovens in the Naramata region, making this the largest concentration of rock ovens in North America.

1. The first four kilometres of this trek travel on part of the Naramata section of the Kettle Valley Railway, so the trail is wide and has a grade of only 1.9 per cent, gaining only 75 m of elevation. It starts out by heading northwest, and almost immediately, views of the lush vineyards of the Naramata plateau are visible below on your left.

2. A sign saying Rock Ovens Park is 13 km away is correct, but the route described here takes a well-marked, and just as well-known, shortcut that bypasses a lot of needless wandering.

3. The first 4 km of the trail are rather uneventful. There are a couple of roads leaving the main trail going up to the right, but the principal route is quite wide and heavily travelled, so it becomes easily apparent which way to go. There is an outhouse on the right about 2 km from the trailhead.

4. At the 4-km mark, again on the right, you will see a sign for Horseshoe Trail. Get onto Horseshoe, which now becomes a rolling, single-track path sending you strolling through sparse forest.

5. In five to seven minutes you will come to Tote Road Trail, veering off to the right. This junction is marked by two signs fastened to trees. One directs you to the right to Tote Road Trail, while the second one steers you to the left to Horseshoe Trail and Rock Oven 7. Take the left (straight) trail, which keeps you on Horseshoe Trail and takes you to Rock Oven 7 in a matter of minutes. These two trails will meet farther up.

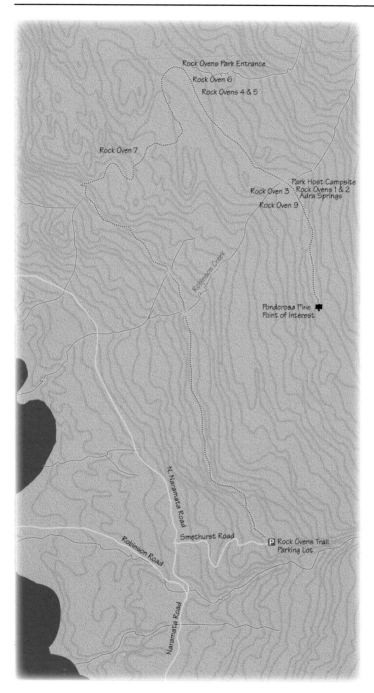

6. After visiting Rock Oven 7, carry on along the trail, watching for the sign that says "Hook-up to Tote Road Trail," and a few minutes later, you will in fact hook up with Tote Road Trail. Continue your journey on Tote Road.

7. The trail through forest will break out to a power line road, ending in a T-junction after about 15 minutes. You have hiked 1.7 km from the main trail and 5.7 km from the trailhead. Turn left onto the power line road. Signs direct you to Tote Rd. and to Tote Road Trail. Either route will deliver you to Rock Ovens Park. For this hike, take Tote Rd., which travels under the power lines.

8. Tote Rd. meets with Track #2 Rd. in 8–10 minutes. You will enter Rock Ovens Park immediately after turning right onto Track #2 Rd.

9. Wander through Rock Ovens Park on this road and explore Rock Ovens 1–6 and 9 for about 30–45 minutes. The ovens are spread out but marked with signage. All of them require a minor hike just off the main road.

10. You are in a park, so there are a couple of amenities, but only a couple. There is an outhouse and a park host campsite.

11. This hike travels 3.6 km on Track #2 Rd., taking in the aforementioned rock ovens, but it also passes the paltry Adra Springs and culminates at a ponderosa pine that is 4.5 m in circumference. This pine is marked as a trailside point of interest.

12. Turn around at the large ponderosa pine and return the same way. If you choose to continue through the park, be aware there is significant additional distance to travel (4–5 km), and then backtracking, to see Rock Ovens 8, 10 and 11.

The entrance to Rock Ovens Park is on a shaded gravel road.

This magnificent ponderosa pine is marked with signage as a point of interest, and is the turnaround point for this trek. This big beauty is worth the extra time to see and enjoy. It has a circumference of 4.5 metres.

The principal attraction on this trek is the rock ovens. Seen here, you can envision the heat that these ovens produced enabling cooks to bake an abundance of bread for railway crews.

Sometimes the journey is just as good as the destination. The beauty of the South Okanagan Valley is appreciated as you hike toward Rock Ovens Park. The top image looks north, the bottom one west across the lake to the town of Summerland.

31. Ellis Ridge Trail

Category: Return
Distance: 10.4 km round trip
Height gain: 227 m
High point: 1204 m
Time: 2.5–3.5 hrs. round trip
Difficulty: Easy
Seasons: Spring, summer, fall
Trailhead coordinates: N49 28.412
W119 30.389

As the namesake suggests, this trek is a beautiful ridge walk paralleling Ellis Creek canyon. Viewing the bottom of the canyon is rare on this hike because it is so far beneath you and the walls are steep. Nonetheless, the hike provides ample sights as it meanders along the ridge.

Directions to trailhead: In Penticton, at the intersection of Government St. and Carmi Ave., drive east on Carmi for 6 km to Beaver Dell Rd. Turn right on Beaver Dell and drive 2.2 km to reach a gravel parking lot on the right side of the road. This is labelled the Garnet Fire Interpretive Site parking lot, but it is also the trailhead for the Ellis Ridge Trail.

1. The journey begins on a broad, flat, gravel path. Immediately into the hike, a narrow unmarked trail departs to the right, leaving the main trail. Take this trail.

2. The path descends briefly as it crosses a seasoned double-track trail. It continues its brief descent over a rocky outcropping to intersect with another narrow path. It is important that you turn left onto this trail. All of this happens quickly at the beginning of the hike, so it is imperative to get these landmarks right.

3. The trail now wanders through an open forest, taking you closer to the ridgeline.

4. Ten minutes into the hike, you will see spectacular views of Penticton and Okanagan Lake.

5. A single signpost with the number "5" on it marks a great place to leave the trail and view the canyon below. This is the only point on this hike where the canyon bottom is readily visible.

6. At the 1.2-km (20-minute) mark of the hike you will come to the only signage on the trail. One sign points you to Canyon View Trail where you just came from, while the other marker sends you leftward to Ellis Ridge Trail. You want to follow Ellis Ridge Trail.

7. As you hike along this ridge walk there will be various vantage points that provide you with good vistas of the canyon walls, but these are indiscriminate and will require some bushwhacking on your part, as there aren't any dedicated trails to the ridge's edge.

8. For over 2 km the trail rolls up and down with many flat spots as it follows and departs from the canyon's slope, but the net result is an increase in elevation.

9. It is at this point that Beaver Dell Rd. comes into view. The trail has been below the road for most of the hike, but at this point, 30–35 minutes from the signs, the gradual elevation gain has brought the path almost up to the altitude of the road. Unfortunately, the trail stays within earshot of the road for the next 20–30 minutes.

10. At the 4.5-km mark there is a fantastic open viewpoint in a patch of grassland that provides wonderful vistas of the hills across the canyon and of the south side canyon walls themselves.

11. The trail comes to an end five minutes later where a gravel road from Beaver

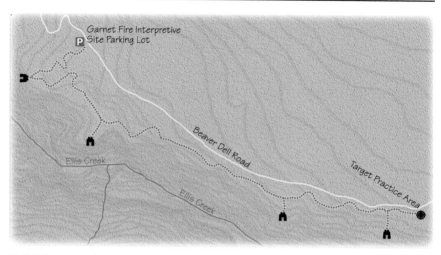

Dell Rd. enters the forest. This road replaces the trail and continues eastward. You can continue to walk this road, but motorized traffic is allowed. This is made most evident by the piles of garbage that have been dumped on the side of the road. Just a few minutes farther up the road brings you to a target practice area as well. I'm all for sharing the great outdoors with everybody, and the outdoors provides a multitude of activities, but I know that most of my readers will agree you should just simply pick up after yourself. The neglect to follow this simple rule is very evident at the target practice area.

12. Return the same way or hike the road back to your vehicle.

Ellis Ridge Trail provides an assortment of sights. In this image the depth of Ellis Creek canyon is demonstrated as you glimpse the west wall of the gorge.

The southernmost shoreline of Okanagan Lake is clearly seen along Ellis Ridge Trail.

Gazing to the northwest from Ellis Ridge Trail, Okanagan Lake extends as far as the eye can see.

As the trek on Ellis Ridge Trail stretches out, many distinctive topographies of the same canyon can take on differing appearances.

32. Oliver Tower Viewpoint

Category: Return
Distance: 2.4 km round trip
Height gain: 261 m
High point: 594 m
Time: 1–2 hrs. round trip
Difficulty: Moderate
Seasons: Spring, summer, late fall
Trailhead coordinates: N49 10.953
W119 33.632

Directions to trailhead: Travel south from Penticton for 41 km to the town of Oliver, where Highway 97 becomes Main St. Turn right (west) onto School Ave. (400 Ave.) and drive 600 m. Then turn left onto Spartan St. (6200 Ave.). Drive 100 m and turn right on Spartan Pl. (6100 Ave.). Go to the end of Spartan Pl. and park on your right in the only parking spot for the trail.

1. The trail begins to ascend right away, taking you through a corral-type fence.

This quick, yet steep hike takes you to a communication tower overlooking the town of Oliver.

The soil here is comprised mainly of sand and fine dirt, so your upward progress is impeded by a lack of traction, much like hiking up a scree slope.

2. This only lasts about five minutes and the loose-soiled hill's grade lessens with solid earth beneath your feet.

3. Ten to twelve minutes into the hike, the trail's grade decreases significantly for about five minutes before becoming steeper once again. This pattern of sharp climbs followed by lesser grades is consistent throughout this trek.

4. Roughly 1 km, or 15–18 minutes, from the start, the trail connects with another trail that approaches the summit from a different starting point. This trail

The town of Oliver seen from the Oliver Tower Viewpoint.

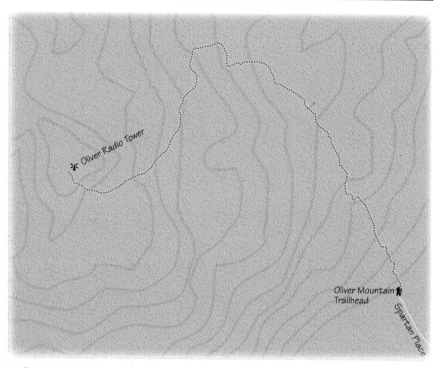

is distinguishable by its width – this is actually an old road. Turn left, upward, onto this road, but only for a few moments.

5. After walking on the road for a short time, you will see a faded single-track trail departing to the left. If you miss this and stay on the road, you will eventually arrive at the ultimate destination anyway, although the road's route is somewhat longer and winds around indiscriminately, making it substantially longer. For the purposes of this trek's description, take the left turn on the aforementioned single-track trail.

6. This route allows for a somewhat leisurely stroll in front of the communication tower, and within 15 minutes you arrive on the west side of the tower.

7. There is a large, elevated wooden platform that is a great spot for erecting your camera tripod or resting your weary muscles.

8. The views of Oliver, the South Okanagan Valley, Tugulnuit Lake and Okanagan River are superb.

*Looking north up the South Okanagan Valley
from the Oliver Tower Viewpoint.*

33. Keremeos Columns

Category: Return
Distance: 11.8 km round trip
Height gain: 660 m
High point: 1178 m
Time: 3–4 hrs. round trip
Difficulty: Moderately strenuous
Seasons: Spring, summer, fall
Trailhead coordinates: N49 13.752
   W119 48.920

The Keremeos Columns are tall, vertical, hexagonal pillars of lava that cooled slowly about 30 million years ago. Standing approximately 30 m high, these basalt columns are a sight that is worth the effort of a long upward hike.

Directions to trailhead: Drive east on Keremeos's main street, 7th Ave., until you reach the flashing amber light where 7th Ave. intersects Highway 3 East. Turn left on Highway 3 East and drive 3.7 km to Liddicoat Rd. on the right side of the highway. Once on Liddicoat Rd., drive for 1 km, looking for a paved parking lot on the left side of the road. Somewhere within this kilometre, Liddicoat Rd. becomes Pincushion Trail (still a paved road), which then intersects with Liddicoat Rd. at the 1-km mark. It seems the residential developers in the area laid down pavement on pre-existing trails, hence the erratic street-naming system. Regardless, the paved parking lot is on the left side, 1 km from Highway 3 East.

1. Like many trails in this region, this one is actually a 4×4 road instead of a traditional trail. The route begins as a short-lived paved road that starts to climb right away. This moderate climb continues for about 40 minutes (2.7 km), before levelling off for a few moments.

2. The road is highly visible from the trailhead as it switchbacks its way up a mountainside toward two separate communication towers, the first of which is 1.6 km from the trailhead.

3. About 25 minutes from trailhead, you will go through a gate, the first of two on this trek. If either one is closed, please close it behind you. At this first gate, the communication towers come into view.

The lower one is on your right, and the upper one is farther up to your left.

4. Ten minutes later, the road goes under a power line just before levelling off for a few minutes.

5. Minor roads enter and exit the main road, but the way is apparent, as the main road is obvious by being the most travelled.

6. There are two forks where it is difficult to distinguish which branch to follow. The first of these is encountered 50 minutes into the hike, the second just 5–10 minutes later. At the first fork, it makes no difference which branch you take, since they rejoin a short distance beyond the fork. The second junction, however, is rather important. Make sure you take the left fork, which will take you upward through open sagebrush. Taking the right-hand one will send you toward a forested gully and an uncertain destination. This second junction is 3.7 km from the trailhead.

7. You will go through the second gate at the 5-km mark. This translates roughly to 1.5 hours from the trailhead, with 56-year-old legs on a steady uphill grade.

8. The remaining 900 m takes about 15–20 minutes to complete, as the uphill grade continues without the distraction of any divergent side roads.

9. As you emerge through a sparse forest at the end of the trail, the columns of basalt tower above you.

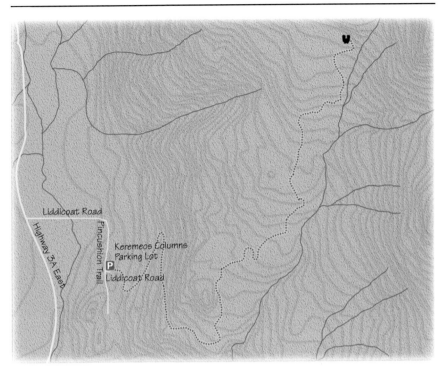

Panoramas are plentiful on the Keremeos Columns trail. Keremeos Creek winds its way south to the Similkameen River.

Land of sage and sun. The parched landscape of the semi-arid South Okanagan is home to the resilient sagebrush and knapweed.

The hike to the Keremeos Columns is an uphill grind. This is about the halfway mark from the valley bottom that is not quite visible below.

*The destination Keremeos Columns
have eroded over several million years,
leaving a pile of rubble at your feet.*

*A closer look at the columns reveals an
intricate, hexagonal, jigsaw-like pattern.*

34. McIntyre Bluff

Category: Return
Distance: 11 km round trip
Height gain: 251 m
High point: 669 m
Time: 2.5–3.5 hrs. round trip
Difficulty: Moderately strenuous
Seasons: Spring, summer, fall
Trailhead coordinates: N49 14.691
  W119 33.297

Although this hike gains 251 m of elevation, it is spread out over a considerable distance, with the moderate elevation gain being interrupted by several level areas. Therefore, this is one of those hikes that delivers you to a generous viewpoint with only moderate exertion.

Directions to trailhead: Drive south on Highway 97 from Penticton toward the town of Oliver. As you enter Oliver from the north, look for Secrest Hill Rd. on the right. Get onto Secrest Hill Rd. and follow it for 1.2 km, where you will turn right onto Covert Pl. Drive a short distance to the Covert Farms parking lot, on your left. The owners and staff are kind enough to permit parking here and allow you to walk on their farmland, as long as you park and walk. They do not like unauthorized vehicles driving around the acreage. It is an 875-m hike from the parking lot to the trailhead.

1. From the parking lot, hike north on the main road, following the "U-pick" and "McIntyre Bluff" signs. Ten minutes from the parking lot, there is an intersection where one sign sends you to the u-pick to the left and to "McIntyre Bluff Entrance" to the right.

2. Soon after you take this right turn, the entrance to the trail appears on the left side of the road through a gate. Much of this area is closed to wildlife by means of a high, electrified wire fence. There is a bounty of grapes and vegetables in the flatlands that could easily be destroyed by hungry deer if precautions were not taken to keep them out. Nonetheless, the gate is not electrified, but please be courteous and close it behind you.

3. The trail splits immediately. Take the right-hand, single-track trail.

4. The trail runs alongside the electrified fence (fence on the right) for about ten minutes before it takes an upward turn to the left at a sign directing you to Rattlesnake Lake. The trail now becomes a wide 4×4 road that climbs moderately through open sage.

5. Seven to eight minutes later the trail goes past a park boundary sign and progresses under power lines for 3–4 minutes.

6. Roughly 25–30 minutes, or 1.5 km, from the gated trailhead, you will come to the second sign directing you to Rattlesnake Lake, to the right. It's a rather odd place for a directional sign, as there isn't a fork in the trail or any discernible way of getting lost. Nevertheless, follow the sign, maintaining the obvious course on the path.

7. Five minutes later, what is presumably Rattlesnake Lake comes into close proximity on your left. There are no markers or signs indicating the name of the lake, but it is the only one encountered on this trek.

8. Just beyond the lake, the trail seeks refuge from the sun, for only about five minutes, in a forest of western hemlock. Look for a sign at a fork in the trail that will send you to the right toward McIntyre Bluff.

9. Soon after you take this fork, another sign will direct you to McIntyre Bluff, but again there is no junction at this sign, so

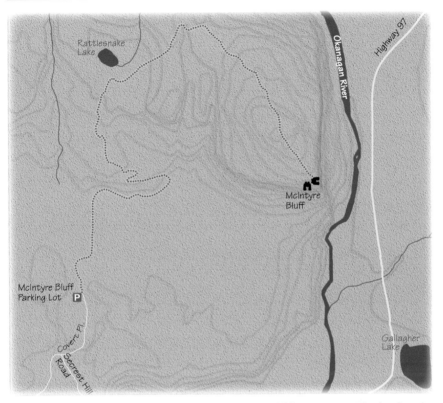

continue straight. At this sign, you have hiked 2.8 km from the gated trailhead and 3.7 km from the parking lot.

10. The next 15–20 minutes consists of an undulating path through a mixture of open forest and open sage.

11. With five to ten minutes to go to reach the summit, yet another directional marker emerges, guiding you upward. There is no junction at this sign either.

12. The sights from the top of the bluff are incredibly immense. The landscapes seen up and down the Southern Okanagan Valley from here are unparalleled. I believe I've spent more time hanging around this summit than any others I've hiked in the entire Okanagan Valley. Vaseux Lake dominates the northern view, while the Okanagan Highland captivates your senses across the Okanagan Valley to the east. The Okanagan River is directly beneath you, making its way south to Osoyoos Lake.

This small pond is "Rattlesnake Lake,"
and is one of a few premium resting
spots on the McIntyre Bluff trek.

*A beautiful vista of Mount Keogan with
Rattlesnake Lake in the foreground on
the way to the summit of McIntyre Bluff.
So much diversity on this hike.*

Yikes! Step back. This picture was snapped while looking directly over the edge of McIntyre Bluff. The Okanagan River and Highway 97 are immediately below.

Vaseux Lake is just a few kilometres north of Secrest Hill Rd. to McIntyre Bluff. This tranquil setting is home to many species of birds, and is a resting area for many migratory waterfowl species as well. There is a boardwalk with viewing platforms on the shoreline, and I recommend you take a few minutes away from the busy highway and relax at this wonderful spot.

The plateaus of the South Okanagan Valley are used primarily for agriculture. Here you can see the cultivated land of Covert Farms.

The Okanagan Valley looking south from the summit of McIntyre Bluff on a blistering hot, hazy Okanagan afternoon.

The use of wind-generated power is becoming increasingly popular. This vineyard at the base of McIntyre Bluff has windmills spotted throughout the acreage.

McIntyre Bluff is easily recognized as you walk toward the trailhead through vineyards on Covert Farms.

35. Golden Mile Stamp Mill Trail

Category: Return with a small loop
   at the mill ruins
Distance: 6 km round trip
Height gain: 162 m
High point: 562 m
Time: 2–3 hrs. round trip
Difficulty: Easy
Seasons: Spring, summer, late fall
Trailhead coordinates: N49 09.026
   W119 35.499

Directions to trailhead: From the town of Oliver, drive south on Highway 97 for a few kilometres to Road 7 on your right. Once on Road 7, follow the signs to Tinhorn Creek Winery. The winery is on private property, but the owners have graciously permitted hiking through their vineyard to access Golden Mile Stamp Mill Trail. They have gone so far as to permit parking for the trail in their busy lot. Please obey all signs and respect private property.

The highlight of this hike is the ruins of an 1890s stamp mill that was once used to process ore that was brought in on railcars. The remainder of the hike is a wonderful, open grassland/ sage hike that travels along a benchland for several kilometres. For the purposes of this trek description, the entire length of the hike is shortened to end at a spectacular viewpoint atop a grassy knoll, as the entire length of the benchland stroll becomes monotonous.

1.   From your vehicle, head up the same road you came in on. About 20–30 m up the road, turn right at the T-junction – you are still on a paved road.

2.   Very quickly you will approach another T-junction, where this time you turn left, following the signs to the stamp mill.

3.   The pavement ends abruptly, and you will stroll along a dirt and gravel road right through the middle of the vineyard. Stay on the main road and do not venture into the vineyard.

4.   Ten minutes from the trailhead, the vineyard ends. Follow the signs directing you to the left.

5.   Up to the right of you is the first of two electrified fences that require crossing. The first one is rather unique. This fence is designed to keep snakes out of the vineyard, so it runs along the ground

and is only about 1 m high. There is a step on both sides of the fence, providing safe clearance.

6.   Soon after crossing the snake fence you will come to a second fence. This one too is electrified, but it is designed to keep larger wildlife out of the vineyard. There is a gate, also electrified, which you can pass through, and the instructions for doing so are posted on the gate and its latch. Please close the gate after you pass through.

7.   From here, the way to the mill is straightforward, as the trail has ample signage. After you pass through the second gate, the approach is uphill for about 8–10 minutes.

8.   A couple of minutes after the trail becomes level, you will come to an intersection where a sign will guide you to the left to the mill. This is the point where the mill loop re-enters the main trail.

9.   The mill ruins come into view on your right as you drop down into a clearing amid a forested area.

10. To obtain a closer look, and loop back to the main trail, follow a faint pathway to the left that goes behind the mill rubble. Continue on this trail to come back to the main trail.

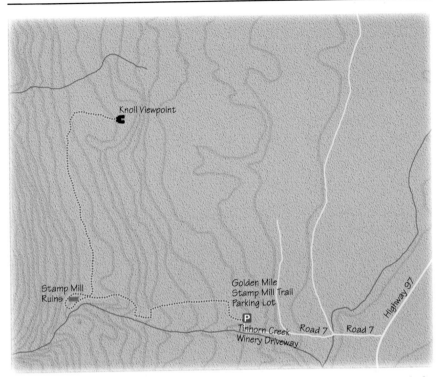

11. Once back at the intersection that completes the loop, turn left onto the main trail. This trail now is actually an old road.

12. Enjoy a pleasant walk through open grasslands, acknowledging and avoiding livestock in the area.

13. The road briefly enters a forest of pine and spruce about 15 minutes, or 1 km, from the mill site.

14. The road opens to expansive grasslands once again after a quick stint through the forest. Although there is not a definitive trail, there is a reasonably high knoll to your right, about 200 m away. Make your way to this knoll for incredible vistas of Osoyoos Lake to the south, while to the southeast lie the Okanagan Highland, the town of Oliver and the sprawling agriculture of the Okanagan Valley.

15. Make your way back the same way you came, forgoing the mill loop.

The stamp mill ruins are the main feature of Golden
Mile Stamp Mill Trail. The mill was used to process ore.

The town of Oliver from a viewpoint
on Golden Mile Stamp Mill Trail.

Useful websites

Kelowna Tourism
www.tourismkelowna.com/do/
activities-attractions/hiking

B.C. Parks
www.env.gov.bc.ca/bcparks

**Regional District of
Okanagan-Similkameen
Trail Search**
www.rdos.bc.ca/index.php?id=140

Acknowledgements

As always, without the support and encouragement of my wife, Debbie, I would still be sitting on the couch, wishing I was outside. Thank you for tolerating my weekend passion, Debbie.